Spice & Ice

Spice & Ice 60 Tongue-Tingling Cocktails **by Kara Newman**

photographs by **Antonis Achilleos**

CHRONICLE BOOKS

SAN FRANCISCO

Library of Congress Cataloging-

in-Publication Data available.

ISBN 978-0-8118-6667-5

Manufactured in China.

Designed by **Vanessa Dina**

Prop and food styling by **spork**

Typesetting by **Janis Reed**

10 9 8 7 6 5 4 3 2 1

Chronicle Books LLC

680 Second Street

San Francisco, California 94107

www.chroniclebooks.com

Acknowledgments

Thank you to . . .

Gretchen VanEsselstyn and the team at *Chile Pepper* magazine
for championing chile-heads everywhere, and for kindly
supporting this project.

Bill LeBlond, Amy Treadwell, Sarah Billingsley, Vanessa Dina,
Ben Kasman, Doug Ogan, David Hawk, and Peter Perez at
Chronicle Books.

Jonathan Lyons, attorney extraordinaire.

All the bartenders, mixologists, and cocktail experts that contributed
recipes, especially Jacques Bezuidenhout, Ryan Magarian, Vanessa
Maruskin, Pichet Ong, Tim Stookey, Adam Seger, Willy Shine, Alex
Urena, Danny Valdez, Phil Ward, and Janet Zimmerman. Apologies
to anyone I've neglected to mention by name; there were so many
inspirations from cocktail menus across the country.

The Astor Center for letting me mix up some of these recipes in a
classroom setting, and proving there was an audience for the book.
And thanks to everyone who took the class—especially those happy
masochists who pressed for the drinks to be *even hotter!* That was a
critical turning point.

My brave band of drink testers (it's a tough job, but someone had to
do it!): Shaun Adams, Ray Asuncion, Mark Basanta, Simon Binder,
Joe Marotta, Sasha "The Mensch" Martens, Joelle Silverman Miller,
Keith Morton, Caroline Pacht, Diana Pittet, Jennifer Sendor, Robert
Silverman, Valerie Rodriguez, Tim Stookey, Darrin Towne, Gretchen
VanEsselstyn, Kevin Whelan, Ya-Roo Yang, and Chris Zawacki (and
apologies for anyone I've missed!). Thanks for lending your Teflon
taste buds and providing thoughtful feedback, support throughout
the book-writing process, and some fantastic drink names. Testing
out drinks with you was helpful and always a blast.

Melkon Khosrovian of Modern Spirits for providing sensible food-
safety guidelines.

David Leite for mentoring me through the book process and telling it
like it is and for inspiring by example.

Andy Smith for always encouraging and supporting me, as he has
with so many other new writers finding their way, and for quietly and
generously offering damn good advice.

Eliott and Naomi Newman; Jennifer and Madelyn Sendor; Alan and
Sandy Silverman; Joelle, Laurie, and Rowana Fay Miller.

Robert Silverman—first, last, and always. Thanks for bragging and
believing.

Dedication

To Robert

TABLE OF CONTENTS

Introduction—Why Spicy Cocktails? 8

Drink Recipes by the Season 50

Resources 153

Index 155

Introduction:

WHY SPICY COCKTAILS?

Spicy cocktails are novel, but they're more than just a novelty. As a columnist for *Chile Pepper* magazine's "High Spirits" column, I was assigned to write about topics such as habanero pepper–infused vodka, cocktail pairings for red-hot barbecue, and super-spicy holiday punches.

At first I fretted that I would have trouble filling column space. Boy, was I wrong. Before long, I realized that a significant number of bars and restaurants had at least one "spicy" drink on cocktail menus to entice adventurous customers and that they tend to sell well. Every mixologist and bar consultant seemed to have a few in his or her repertoire. And during my recipe-testing phases, friends were unusually eager to help try the drinks—they were fun, different, conversation pieces. There was more to write about than I'd ever imagined.

In the course of the happy research for my column, I learned two important lessons. First: Heat alone does not make a great drink. But a carefully crafted spicy drink hits all the right flavor notes and leaves a pleasant, faintly glowing heat on the lips and tongue, creating an excitement for the next sip.

Unfortunately, I've been the victim of bubble gum–flavored Cosmos with a shriveled jalapeño tossed on top, a misguided attempt to enliven a stale bar menu. The end result was neither fresh nor enjoyable to drink and underscored that spice alone is not enough. Like any drink, a spicy cocktail should use fresh ingredients—seasonal if at all possible, which is why this book is divided into four seasons. Flavors and heat levels need to be balanced and not too crazy hot or, at the other end of the spectrum, too weak and faintly bitter.

And second: A turbo-charged cocktail gone wrong can be a *very* painful mistake! Too much Tabasco in a Bloody Mary or a vodka infusion with a cut serrano left in too long means your next party will end abruptly, guests yelping, eyes watering as they flee. It's critical to balance cocktails in terms of both flavor and heat levels. And that requires some guidance and practice.

Even if you're the rare drinker with Teflon taste buds, there's one cardinal rule for crafting spicy drinks. It's not about creating a flame-out of a drink—it's about finding the right balance of heat. Master mixologist Jacques Bezuidenhout, who created the award-winning Tabasco-spiked One Hot Minute cocktail, summed it up best: "You have to be able to finish the drink and still want another one."

In the interest of readers, I asked professional bartenders, "What's the ratio of cayenne pepper to paprika to rim a martini glass?" "Is it better to use whole or sliced jalapeños to infuse a bottle of tequila?" "How do you cool down a drink if the heat gets too intense?" This book aims to provide guidelines for making drinks with just the right amount of lip-tingling heat, as well as a few guidelines for toning down spice to adjust your drink, and as a last resort, tips for cooling the burn when that's needed.

But when we get it just right, spicy cocktails are fun and make us feel good. Some liken the capsaicin rush to an athlete's endorphin high. Sometimes, all that's needed is a tiny drop of Tabasco to add gentle warmth to an otherwise standard margarita recipe—the equivalent of the afterglow from a feel-good run in the park. Other times, the goal is a fiery sizzle, made by adding a daring handful of crushed habaneros to a party punch—not unlike the extreme adrenaline rush of a daredevil skydiving adventure. This is why we become hooked on spicy foods—we love the endorphin rush!

Let's get one common misconception out of the way: "spice" doesn't always equal Scoville units. Some spices—hot and sweet paprika, anise, and cinnamon, for example—add bursts of flavor rather than heat.

Spice & Ice is about finding those bold bursts of flavor and using heat and spice to frame fresh ingredients in a glass, showing them off to best advantage. Spicy drinks can be crazy, they can be elegant—but above all, they have to be delicious!

THE ELEMENTS OF SPICE

THE SPECTRUM OF COCKTAIL FLAVORS
As a cocktail enthusiast, most likely you already know that there's a wide range of cocktail flavors. Where do spicy drinks fit in?

Sweet/fruity: At one end of the spectrum, you have sweet and fruit-driven cocktails, like daiquiris and Cosmopolitans, and these are the types of flavors that are most frequently associated with cocktails. Done well, sweet/fruity potions are pleasing and easy to drink; done poorly, they tend to be syrupy, sickly-sweet concoctions.

Herbal/floral: The next category can be characterized as herbal or floral. Gin drinks, such as classic martinis and gin and tonics, fall easily within this group, especially considering the wide range of botanicals used in gin. But I also think of cocktails made with light floral elements, such as elderflower, or those with delicate, fragrant characteristics, such as tea-based drinks.

Bitter: After that, I look to bitter cocktails—the Negroni is a classic example. Drinks made with liqueurs such as Campari, Aperol, or Cynar can be an acquired taste (as can some spicy drinks), although they also may have sweet or herbaceous notes to round out the drink. (I think also of drinks with sweet overtones that use bitters to add complexity and balance as sometimes spanning categories.)

Savory: And then we get to savory drinks, a fast-rising category in the drinks world. While the Bloody Mary is the most obvious drink in this category, an increasing number of bartenders are moving the needle away from sweet drinks and toward savory contenders made with vegetables (such as tomatoes, carrots, or cucumbers) and herbs (like basil and mint) rather than fruit juices.

As you go through this book, you'll notice that all of the above categories are represented. That's because spiced and spicy drinks can span across categories, adding interest and punch, without obscuring the characteristics of the cocktails we love. But spicy cocktails deserve their own category as well:

Spiced: Spiced cocktails may have a touch of heat or no heat at all. Think of mulled apple cider, enriched with cinnamon, cloves, and nutmeg as a great representation. The spices are a critical part of what makes the drink rich and appealing; without their complexity and zing, warm cider can be pretty ordinary.

Spicy: Hot and spicy cocktails run the gamut from piquant to downright incendiary! These are the cocktails infused with chile peppers, hot sauces, wasabi, and so on, providing a lift to sweet, herbal, bitter, and savory drinks. Spice and heat alone are not what make a cocktail great—but balanced with other flavors, they elevate a drink to a delicious and exciting experience. That's what this book is all about.

Sweet	Daiquiri
Fruity	**Cosmopolitan**
Herbal/Floral	Gin and Tonic
Bitter	Negroni
Savory	Bloody Mary
Spiced	**Mulled Cider**
Spicy!	**Dragonfire**

SPICY DO'S AND DON'TS

A few quick tips to keep in mind as you learn how to work with spicy ingredients.

Do:

Keep flavors balanced. Heat alone does not make a great drink. As you try out recipes from this book and experiment with your own variations, use spicy ingredients to enhance and play off the other flavors in your drink.

Wear gloves if you're cutting hot peppers. Gloves are a small but important precaution to take, especially when working with habaneros, serranos, and other peppers on the hotter end of the scale. Exposure to chiles—especially oils from the seeds—can irritate cuts or abrasions on your hands.

Start with less heat. You can always add more! It's difficult (but not impossible) to abate heat by adding more juice, sugar, or cream to a recipe. But especially if you're making a single drink, it seems wasteful to make a larger portion than you had intended, and it can throw your whole drink out of balance. Start with a couple of drops of hot sauce and taste your drink. Add a little more if the heat level needs more intensity.

Don't:

Use shriveled old peppers. Fresh is best. Just as you shop for the freshest fruits and vegetables, apply the same standards to chile peppers. Younger peppers tend to have more heat and flavor. Look for vibrant color and glossy, smooth skins (except for poblano peppers, which are naturally a bit wrinkly).

Assume guests can handle heat. It's tempting to show off an extreme cocktail to impress guests, but not everyone enjoys spicy food or cocktails. For parties, consider serving drinks with and without spice-rimmed glasses, or let guests rim their own glasses for fun.

Rub eyes after cutting peppers—ouch! Trust me on this one. Remove your gloves and wash your hands thoroughly before touching your eyes, nose, or anywhere else on your face. Should you carelessly forget, flush the affected area with cold water or apply a cold compress. Although it won't cause permanent damage, it sure can sting!

TOO HOT! TOO HOT! HOW TO COOL THINGS DOWN

This leads right into the next subject: What steps do you take if your cocktail is just too fiery? You can make a swan dive for that pitcher of ice water. This may numb the burn temporarily, but it won't make it go away. In fact, the water just spreads the capsaicin around your mouth, which can make the heat worse. Instead, reach for one of the following:

A glass of milk or a hunk of cheese. Dairy products coat your mouth and throat and cool the burn fast. This is why sour cream is such a popular accompaniment with spicy Mexican dishes.

Bread. Chewing on a hunk of bread helps; a chunk of bread with cheese is even more effective. When testing out spicy drinks on friends, I usually order in pizza for a casual group or set out a platter of bread, cheeses, and fruit for fancier get-togethers.

A spoonful of sugar. I learned this from pitmaster Mike Mills over at 17th Street Bar & Grill in Murphysboro, Illinois. "If you ever get something in your mouth that's super-hot and burning you up, just get a little pack of sugar and put it on your tongue," Mills counsels. "It smooths it out and takes away the burn." This also applies to cocktail chemistry: Pepper-infused liquor always will be hotter than pepper-infused simple syrup, which mutes heat.

SPICY COCKTAIL AND FOOD PAIRINGS

Just as wine is enhanced by certain foods, the same holds true for cocktail and food pairings. Spicy cocktails work especially well with the following foods:

Fatty foods—cheeses, steak, salmon fillet. Spicy cocktails tend to be more acidic than nonspicy counterparts, which is what makes them perfect for standing up to the marbled fat of a steak or a rich fish like salmon or tuna. At the same time, the fat content in meats and cheeses will temper the heat in the drink.

Seafood—shrimp, scallops, oysters. Choose carefully, but drinks with clean flavors and a hint of heat (such as the Gunpowder Gimlet, the Mule Kick, or the Cajun Martini) make a fine accompaniment for briny fresh oysters or shrimp scampi. (If fried seafood is on the menu, see the following.)

Fried foods—calamari, mozzarella sticks. If fried foods are your weakness, spicy drinks on the fruity and sweet side will fit right in. Try the Spiced Tangerine Caipirinha or the Blackberry-Poblano Margarita with decadent greasy finger foods.

Rich desserts—bread pudding, cheesecake. Chocolate desserts are a natural with spicy drinks (think Mexican Hot Chocolate or spiced coffee drinks). But in general, the richer the dessert, the easier it is to pair with spicy drinks. Another alternative: Choose a dessert-like drink such as the Gingered Apple cocktail or the Fireside, and skip dessert altogether!

Spicy foods—don't bother; pair with cooling cocktails, wine, or beer. This may be surprising, but I *don't* recommend pairing spicy food with spicy drinks. It dilutes the impact of having one or the other. Besides, most people want a cooling beer, lemonade, or icy (but not spicy) Margarita to guzzle alongside a bowl of fiery chili or atomic-level chicken wings.

AN INTRODUCTION TO SPICE CATEGORIES

Open a cocktail menu at any bar or restaurant, and odds are you'll find at least one spicy cocktail featured. This wasn't the case 5, 10, 15 years ago. So why now?

The short answer is that jaded consumers are demanding newer, fresher, more interesting drinks . . . and capable and innovative bartenders are delivering just that. We also can thank our local greenmarkets for better and bolder drinks. The prominence of fresh, locally sourced ingredients means that zesty ingredients such as a wide variety of fresh chile peppers; muddled fresh herbs; and newly ground, extra-pungent spices are available more than ever before.

And while we are drinking locally, we are thinking globally—and the global table is extending to the bar. Creative cocktailians schooled in Indian, Thai, and Latin American cuisines are bringing the traditional spices, sauces, and other ingredients of their world cultures to beverages as well as food dishes. The results are often startling, refreshing, and hot.

So, lucky us, we have a wonderful array of spicy drinks to choose from at the bar, and even more to make at home.

CHOOSING THEM AND USING THEM

This section provides an overview of the spicy ingredients that can be used to pep up cocktails, including fresh, dried, or powdered hot peppers; hot sauces, horseradish, and wasabi; familiar pantry-staple spices like ginger and cloves; and exotic flavors borrowed from cuisines from around the world.

Chile Peppers

Using them: Drop peppers into a bottle of liquor or simple syrup to infuse it with fresh flavor and heat; leave spicier varieties whole, cut less spicy peppers for faster infusion. If you don't have time to infuse a bottle, sliced or diced peppers can be muddled at the bottom of the cocktail shaker—then shake and strain out the pepper pieces for smooth drinking. And don't underestimate the decorative uses of peppers—larger peppers can be cut into attractive rounds and perched on the side of a glass; small peppers can be dropped into a glass whole or speared along with an olive or cucumber slice on a toothpick to garnish.

Choosing them: Chile peppers span a wide range of colors, sizes, and heat levels. In general, the smaller the pepper, the hotter it will be. Some of the commonly available chile peppers I've used in this book are:

- **Jalapeño:** a medium pepper with mild to moderate heat

- **Serrano:** a small, thin, hot pepper

- **Habanero:** a small, squat orange variety with blazing heat

- **Chipotle:** a smoked red chile pepper with medium heat and an earthy flavor

Varieties will differ depending on where you live. I encourage you to try out Anaheim peppers and tiny bird's-eye or Thai peppers. Feel free to substitute what is available with the peppers suggested in this book.

As with any fruit or vegetable, look for smooth, glossy skins and bright colors. Older peppers will lose some of their heat. Keep in mind also that peppers have their season—they usually peak in autumn and can become extremely hot. Recipes using chiles may have to be adjusted seasonally. Cut off a tiny piece and taste it to gauge the heat before adding it to a cocktail; you may need to use more or less than a recipe recommends. (Have a glass of milk ready in case it's too hot!)

Sources: In addition to your local supermarket and green-markets, www.ranchogordo.com ships fresh chile peppers in season and dried chiles year-round. Or if you have a green thumb, try growing your own peppers: www.chileplants.com is a super resource for live plants. There's also a mind-boggling chile chart listing hundreds of pepper varieties, as well as their heat levels and country of origin.

Learning Your Chile Peppers

This is just a brief overview of the chile pepper kingdom. Entire books have been devoted to understanding the chile universe if you're so inclined. According to Gretchen VanEsselstyn, editor in chief of *Chile Pepper* magazine, the following books are "the most used books on our reference shelf":

Peppers of the World: An Identification Guide by Dave DeWitt and Paul W. Bosland

The Chile Pepper Encyclopedia by Dave DeWitt

Peppers: The Domesticated Capsicums by Jean Andrews

Hot Peppers, Dried and Powdered

Using them: A multitude of dried whole and powdered peppers are available. Whole dried peppers can be saturated in vodka or another liquor to help flavor and add heat, but they can also add unwanted bitterness and may not hold heat. I recommend using fresh peppers whenever possible. However, powders are another story: chipotle, ancho, cayenne, paprika, and chili powders are phenomenal additions to your spicy cocktail arsenal. Use them to rim glasses—either solo or paired with salt, sugar, or cocoa—to punch up an otherwise ordinary drink, or sprinkle a dash on top of a martini to create a "gunpowder" effect. Pepper powders also work well stirred into hot drinks, dissolving into Mexican Hot Chocolate or a spicy coffee concoction.

Choosing them: Like other spices, check regularly to make sure your pepper powders have retained their heat, flavor, and pungency. Toss anything that has changed color or flavor.

Hot Sauces

Using them: Marinate cocktail olives, green beans, or onions in them, or add a few dashes to an icy-cold drink for a splash of heat and color.

Choosing them: New Orleans–made Tabasco is a standard for Bloody Mary–style tomato-based drinks, but there are also standbys like Tabasco (red or green), Louisiana Hot, or any other hot sauce that stirs your taste buds and your imagination. Consider hot sauces from different continents—for example, Thai Sriracha sauce, Portuguese piri-piri sauce, Peruvian *aji rocoto* pepper sauce, or locally produced specialties.

Another option: Editor in Chief Gretchen VanEsselstyn turned me on to a clear hot sauce, Frostbite, which seems custom made for adding heat to drinks without adding color.

Horseradish

Using it: Remember—a little goes a long way. Wasabi powder, a staple from Japanese cooking, stirred into vodka or sake adds instant punch and a lovely light green hue, while fresh horseradish can be peeled and allowed to infuse for long periods or grated to add sinus-clearing pungency to drinks. Meanwhile, radishlike daikon can be juiced and added to *shochu* for a delicate tang. Since bottled horseradish may have vinegar or other strong flavors added in, save it for drinks with equally strong flavors to balance it out.

Choosing it: Select powdered wasabi, rather than paste, for easier mixing into drinks. It will keep nearly indefinitely. Horseradish root is ugly and surprisingly hard to find; I can only guess that the convenience and ubiquity of bottled horseradish has edged out the fresh stuff, but freshly grated horseradish root elevates Bloody Mary–style drinks to a new level. A bit of hard-won advice on grating horseradish: Use a food processor, not a hand grater, or you'll be crying for days!

Ethnic Ingredients

Using them: Let spices and sauces from other countries and cultures inspire drinks, such as the Tandoori Sunrise, which is rimmed with Indian spices like turmeric and cumin, or the Bangkok Margarita, which features a dusting of exotic Aleppo pepper from Syria.

Choosing them: The seasoning you choose can be used to inspire creative cocktails from Asia (wasabi, Sriracha) and the Caribbean (fresh nutmeg, jerk seasonings). Keep in mind that a little will go a long way—try to keep drinks balanced.

Peppercorns

Using them: When it comes to cocktails, peppercorns are best used sparingly. Black peppercorns can be a fine way to add visual interest to a drink, whether ground over the top of an otherwise sweet cocktail that needs a bit of edge or used to rim a glass. I found during the process of testing drinks that it's easy for peppered drinks to translate as gritty and sneezy rather than spicy. If you are using peppercorns, make sure they are cracked well or ground well. Whole peppercorns at the bottom of a cocktail tend to make a nasty surprise.

Choosing them: Black, white, and pink peppercorns should be part of your pantry as well as your bar.

"Not So Hot" Spices

Using them: All of these elements can be used to infuse simple syrups, tinctures, or liquors. Ginger, lemongrass, or fresh leafy herbs can be muddled at the bottom of a cocktail glass with a bit of sugar to coax out additional flavor. A dash of powdered spices (cinnamon, clove, etc.) also can be sprinkled on the top of a drink for additional aroma, and whole spices like cinnamon sticks and star anise make beautiful (but not edible) garnishes. Whole nutmeg can be quickly grated on the top of coffee or eggnog drinks using a handheld grater or microplane for extra flavor and fragrance.

Choosing them: Be sure to use fresh spices for peak aroma and pungency; any old, stale bottles of spices with no fragrance or flavor should be tossed. Rule of thumb is to replace spices every three months.

The Joy of Ginger

Ginger is a spicy cocktail enthusiast's best friend and a great way to ease non-chile-head friends into the realm of exotic drinks. Powdered ginger has its place, but there's nothing like fresh ginger root to give drinks a bit of zing, without aggressive chile pepper–style heat. Knobby ginger root is available at most grocery stores. Find a piece that doesn't appear to be dried out or withered, take it home, and peel it and cut it into coin-size pieces to muddle in a drink or use for creating infused alcohol. Candied ginger, speared on a toothpick and balanced on the rim of a glass, also makes a tasty garnish. (Or gild the lily by dipping an edge in dark chocolate.) Ginger is also one of the rare elements with the versatility to span all the seasons—it's refreshing and cooling in summer drinks, yet warming and welcoming in winter gingerbread–inspired libations, too.

THE SPICY LIQUOR CABINET

Let me begin by telling you what this chapter is *not*: It's not a comprehensive guide to every kind of liquor and liqueur under the sun. (If that's what you're looking for, I'm happy to direct you to Gary Regan's *The Bartender's Bible* or any of the other excellent books published on the subject.)

Rather, this is a view of the world liquor cabinet through the eyes of a chile-head. Yes, I'm going to tell you all about which liquors are best for infusing and boozing. But let's also look at some wonderful liquors with "bite," which stand up just fine on their own merits without the benefit of spicy additives.

Don't feel the need to instantly acquire every liquor on the following pages. The novice chile-head might want to start with a small selection of vodka and tequila, since both are easy to infuse and blend well into a wide range of cocktails. Add a couple of liqueurs in flavors you enjoy—orange liqueurs are a staple; ginger or allspice liqueurs also are pleasing and interesting additions to drinks. And finish with a bottle of something sweet and suitable for after-dinner sipping, like cognac or a coffee liqueur.

Vodka

Without doubt, vodka is one of the best and easiest liquors to blend with spicy elements. It's like a chameleon; it picks up whatever flavors you add, almost changing its own character in the process. It's also the number-one alcohol sold with flavors added by commercial distillers, and if you can get your hands on a commercial pepper-infused vodka that you like, my advice is to stock up, since specialty flavors often have limited distribution and can disappear from the shelves faster than you can say "Peter Piper picked a peck of chile peppers."

Some good ones to try: Mazama Pepper vodka (Gretchen VanEsselstyn, my editor at *Chile Pepper*, recommended it), and Modern Spirits Celery Peppercorn vodka, which is a natural for Bloody Mary–style drinks. I've heard good things about a chipotle-infused vodka from an American distiller; I think I saw it once at my favorite liquor store and now I can't find it anywhere, even online. I'm starting to think it's an urban myth.

If you can't acquire a bottle of good commercially infused vodka, by all means make your own. The vegetal flavors of hot peppers, Peppadew or other marinated peppers, olives, and other ingredients will remain bright and distinct.

Tequila

Tequila is my second-favorite liquor to use in spicy drinks. You have to work really hard to ruin a margarita; it blends magnificently with spicy flavors. Tequila also makes for a splendid infusion with jalapeños or other hot peppers; it becomes mellow and smoky where vodka stays true and bright.

A few tips on tequila: First, smart bartenders look for tequila made with 100 percent agave (the fermented sap of the weber blue agave plant). Second, get to know the different age classifications of tequila. Silver, or *blanco*, tequila is not aged at all and has peppery, true flavors. *Reposado* (Spanish for "rested"), is aged for 2 to 11 months, usually in an oak barrel. Reposado is usually heavier than blanco tequila, and you'll find both used in cocktails (sometimes in combination). *Añejo* (aged) tequila has been aged for 1 to 3 years, developing a richer, more intense flavor. Sometimes it's subbed for whiskey or bourbon in cocktails (try the Añejo Manhattan); other times it's sipped neat or on the rocks, as is *muy añejo* (very aged) tequila.

Gin
Much as I enjoy a good gin and tonic, gin can be challenging to combine into a spicy cocktail. Gin is a neutral spirit and picks up heat easily, but spice can clash with the botanicals that make gin so lovely and refreshing.

Infusing gin with hot peppers takes a light touch. I've had success with mild jalapeños, but hotter peppers like habaneros can overpower gin's delicacy, and I use them sparingly, even muting them with sugar syrup in the Gin and Tonic with Spiced Ice cocktail (page 101). However, ginger is a perfect match with gin, especially gins with a big juniper profile (like Tanqueray). Chilled well, gin martinis also can be sassed up with a "gunpowder" dash of cayenne or dosed with olives marinated in Tabasco.

Although most gins tend toward the citrus, juniper, or floral families, fiery cocktail enthusiasts may enjoy experimenting with pungent gins with a peppery profile, such as Blackwood's Gin, or those with a strong note of cardamom, like Aviation.

Rum
Some of the things the thinking drinker will want to know: Rum is classified as light (young), gold (aged in oak barrels between 3 and 10 years), and dark. Generally, darker rums are aged longer, although sometimes a dark color signifies only

that more caramel color has been added. Light rums are most commonly used in cocktails.

Within the Caribbean, where most rum is made, several unique production styles coexist. Spanish-speaking islands, such as Puerto Rico, are known for lighter rums, while English-speaking islands, such as Jamaica and Barbados, produce fuller-bodied versions with more molasses character. Meanwhile, the French-speaking islands are best known for agricultural rum (*rhum agricole*), which is produced exclusively from sugarcane juice.

Whew! Still with me? Then you'll also want to know about spiced rum, which is made by the addition of spices and sometimes caramel and vanilla flavoring. Captain Morgan is probably the best known in this category, but true chile-heads likely will find it on the tame side. Luckily, it's also easy to make your own spiced rum. Muddled hot peppers and warm spice-infused simple syrups meld nicely with light rum.

Scotch, Whiskey, Bourbon, and Rye

Purists will frown on my lumping all of these liquors together, but I have the same view on all four: they are phenomenal mixed with spicy ingredients and carry a good bite when sipped alone.

In fact, one of my favorite drinks is the Scotch Bonnet—Scotch infused with habanero peppers and mixed together with pineapple juice. I had been nervous that infusing a good Scotch would ruin it, but it only made it better. Bourbon, too, proved remarkably versatile for autumn drinks, balancing out a smoky chipotle-orange syrup, or raspberry spiked with chili powder.

Brandy/Cognac

If you've got a fabulous cognac, by all means save it for your after-dinner snifter. But there's a place for brandy drinks in this book, especially during the colder months, when the alcohol warms to cinnamon and clove essences. I've also become something of an evangelist for Domaine de Canton, a ginger-infused cognac with a low but pleasant heat and a gorgeous frosted-glass bottle. I've doled out petite shots of Domaine de Canton at the beginning of classes to break the ice and ease students into the concept of spicy drinks. It works every time.

Cordials/Liqueurs

This is a potentially huge category. First off, let's talk about cinnamon schnapps. De Kuyper used to have a super-spicy version called Hot Damn! Cinnamon Schnapps. It has all but disappeared off the market, so do your fellow chile-head cocktail enthusiasts a favor and lobby to have it brought back. In the meantime, I've been using Goldschlager as a passable stand-in. The only catch is that every time I break out the bottle, people seem to revert to college age and decide they want to do shots.

Unfortunately, you won't find any spicy liqueurs on the market. But a number of liqueurs have assertive and interesting flavors and are worth trying alone: Licor 43, for example; Sambuca, Pernod, and now-legal absinthe, which all have their own version of a powerful anise dose; St. Elizabeth Allspice Dram (a.k.a. pimento dram); bitters like artichoke-flavored Cynar and the bitter-orange lilt of Aperol.

And even the sweeter liqueurs—triple sec and Cointreau, Kahlúa, crème de cacao, Baileys, and so forth—all add flavor and balance to spicy drinks, so keep adding to your collection and add them judiciously to your cocktail shaker.

MAKING YOUR OWN SPICY INGREDIENTS

An array of spicy infused liquors and syrups allows you to personalize your cocktail creations and take them to the next level. As I've mentioned in the previous chapter, there are very few good, spicy liqueurs and syrups out on the market, although some are starting to creep in. But the only way to get variety—and a degree of control over flavors and heat levels—is to do it yourself.

Of course, what you stock (or make) for your spicy bar is certainly a matter of taste, but a beginning spicy bartender might find it most useful to have on hand a pepper-infused vodka, an infused tequila (perhaps using a different type of pepper), and a spice-infused simple syrup (try a mix of cinnamon and clove). This versatile trio can be used in a multitude of recipes.

HOW TO MAKE SPICE-INFUSED LIQUORS AND SYRUPS AND MORE

Infusing liquor is a straightforward technique. Essentially, it involves throwing flavorful ingredients into a container of liquor and allowing it to steep. The tricky part is figuring out how long to keep the liquor infusing, but after you've finished the process, infused liquor will keep almost indefinitely.

You can add ingredients directly to a bottle of liquor, but an easier method is to pour the liquor into a wide-mouthed jar and then add your chosen ingredients. Seal it tightly and allow it to sit for as little as a couple of hours or as long as a couple of days, tasting occasionally to check for strength and taste. When you've hit the right flavor and heat, remove the spices and use a funnel (and a strainer if needed) to return the now-infused liquor to the original bottle. Close the bottle well and keep it in a cool, dark area as you would any other bottle of prized liquor. Be sure to label it to avoid surprises later on!

If you're convinced that you'll never use a whole bottle of infused liquor, pour a cup or two of the plain alcohol into a smaller container with a lid (such as a small Mason jar) and use that to steep and store your infusion. Keep in mind that smaller amounts of liquor will infuse faster, so you'll probably need to check on your infusion more frequently.

A word of advice: Don't forget to remove the peppers or strain out the spices you've used to infuse. Otherwise the heat level will grow more intense, and ingredients left floating in the alcohol can pickle, or simply go rancid, ruining your results. I once went to a bar renowned for its extreme jalapeño tequila and was shocked when the bartender poured out shots from a jar of nearly green liquid, with unappetizing khaki peppers floating inside. It smelled nasty, too!

Here are some guidelines and recipes for infusing a base liquor. All of these infusions can be used to make the cocktails listed in this book. But feel free to swap in tequila for vodka and serranos for habaneros, and to add ingredients you like and subtract ingredients you hate. Like all recipes, these are intended to be a guide, not a mandate.

A Note on Food Safety

If you want to learn how to cook, go ask a chef. But if you want to know how to make cocktail ingredients, who better to ask than a master distiller? So I had a chat with Melkon Khosrovian, cofounder of the Modern Spirits brand and a master vodka maker.

According to Khosrovian, here's what you need to do to ensure that you're making a safe and hygienic liquor infusion.

1. Wash thoroughly the ingredient(s) for infusing.

2. Infuse using liquor that is at least 25 percent alcohol, or 50 proof. "Nothing living will survive that," Khosrovian assured me.

3. Don't infuse the same alcohol more than twice (i.e., adding more fruit to strengthen the flavor). Start a new batch.

And if you're trying to infuse a simple syrup, Khosrovian says not to worry: "Sugar and salt are great preservatives."

In fact, he considers oxidation to be a greater concern than bacteria in making infused liquors and syrups. While oxidation isn't harmful—the way apples turn brown when they are exposed to the air is a result of oxidation—it can affect appearance and taste.

"It won't taste right," Khosrovian warned. "But that's more a matter of quality rather than safety." How to avoid oxidation? Make sure your ingredients are completely immersed in the liquid; mix or shake the bottle if you see ingredients rising above the water level.

Infused Liquor

Each recipe makes 2 cups of infused alcohol, enough to make four to six cocktails.

JALAPEÑO-INFUSED TEQUILA

Use any type of hot pepper that pleases you. I find that jalapeños add just the right amount of heat for my taste, as well as a note of fresh flavor. Cutting the peppers will allow a faster and hotter infusion; keep them whole for a slower steep. Try this in The Cinder or the Blood Orange–Jalapeño Margarita cocktails.

2 CUPS TEQUILA, PREFERABLY SILVER OR REPOSADO TEQUILA

1 TO 2 HOT PEPPERS, WASHED AND CUT LENGTHWISE

Combine the ingredients in a small container with a lid. Steep for as little as 2 hours or as long as 2 days, until desired heat is achieved. Strain with a fine-mesh sieve and cover tightly.

HORSERADISH-INFUSED VODKA

Adding horseradish-spiked vodka to a Bloody Mary, which often is mixed with fresh or bottled horseradish, creates a double-barreled punch!

2 CUPS VODKA

1 TABLESPOON CLEANED AND CHOPPED FRESH HORSERADISH ROOT

Combine the ingredients in a small container with a lid. Steep for as little as 2 hours or as long as 2 days, until desired pungency is achieved. Strain with a fine-mesh sieve and cover tightly.

CHIPOTLE-INFUSED RUM

When chile peppers are smoked, they become chipotles.
Although I've used dried chipotles to add a smoky warmth
to rum, you can use canned ones, too, but avoid chipotles
marinated in tomato juice.

2 CUPS LIGHT RUM

1 TO 2 CHIPOTLE PEPPERS

Combine the ingredients in a small container with a lid. Steep for as
little as 2 hours or as long as 2 days, until desired flavor and strength
is achieved. Strain with a fine-mesh sieve and cover tightly.

JALAPEÑO-INFUSED VODKA

This versatile workhorse lends punch to virtually any recipe
that calls for vodka, without overpowering other flavors. If
jalapeños are unavailable, substitute serrano or habanero
peppers.

2 JALAPEÑO PEPPERS

ONE 750 ML BOTTLE VODKA

Add the jalapeño peppers to the vodka. Allow it to steep for as little as
2 hours or as long as 2 days. (Taste a spoonful to test the heat level.)
When desired spiciness is achieved, remove the peppers from the bottle.

ROSEMARY AND CITRON–INFUSED VODKA

Herb infusions are a wonderful, fragrant addition to the arsenal and great for serving guests who "don't do" hot and spicy. Add this to lemonade or cranberry juice and garnish with a decorative sprig of rosemary.

2 CUPS VODKA

1 PIECE LEMON PEEL

1 ROSEMARY SPRIG

Combine the vodka and lemon peel in a small container with a lid. Gently roll the rosemary between your palms to bruise the leaves and release its fragrant oils. Then add it to the container. Cover tightly and allow to steep for 2 hours or longer. Strain with a fine-mesh sieve.

SPICED RUM (BASIC)

Commercial spiced rums abound, but makers are mysterious about which spices are in the liquor, and some of the rums taste downright artificial. Making your own yields a clean, zingy result that you can adjust to your personal preference.

ONE 3-INCH PIECE VANILLA BEAN, OR 1 TEASPOON PURE VANILLA EXTRACT

3 CINNAMON STICKS

1 STAR ANISE

2 WHOLE CLOVES

1 PIECE ALLSPICE (OR A PINCH OF GROUND ALLSPICE)

1 WHOLE NUTMEG, CRUSHED

ONE 750 ML BOTTLE GOLD RUM

Add all of the spices to the rum. Close and let steep for 24 hours or as long as 1 week. Strain with a fine-mesh sieve and cover tightly. Use in your favorite rum-based cocktails.

SPICED RUM (ADVANCED)

This unorthodox and more intense version of spiced rum is loosely based on the house-made version found at the Waldorf-Astoria's Peacock Alley bar, where they shake this rum with Cointreau and raspberry puree.

½ FUJI APPLE, DICED

5 COIN-SIZE PIECES PEELED FRESH GINGER

1 DRIED FIG

1 PIECE ORANGE PEEL

1 TABLESPOON BLACK PEPPERCORNS, CRUSHED

ONE 750 ML BOTTLE GOLD RUM

Add all the spices to the rum. Close and let steep for 24 hours or as long as 1 week. Strain with a fine-mesh sieve and cover tightly. Use in your favorite rum-based cocktails.

Simple Syrups

Although there's nothing wrong with using sugar, making simple syrup is easy and worth mastering, especially since you can quickly expand into spiced simple syrups. In addition to creating unusual and memorable cocktails, simple syrups are fabulous for making special nonalcoholic beverages. Refrigerated, most syrups will last about three weeks. (After this, the flavor will start to taste "off," but it won't ferment or otherwise spoil.) Plain simple syrup lasts indefinitely.

There are some good prefab simple syrups out there. Monin does a line of spicy syrups as well as the usual suspects (vanilla, caramel, passion fruit, etc.). Orgeat (almond) syrup and a good, ruby-colored (not hot pink) grenadine are worth having on hand. But choose flavored syrups carefully; avoid the sickly-sweet, neon-colored, artificial flavor–laden versions, which can ruin an otherwise good drink. Better yet, create your own. They are very easy to make and a great way to customize your cocktails.

To infuse syrups, you can use the same peppers and other ingredients that you would use to infuse liquor. However, since sugar tempers spice, you'll notice that syrups will be more muted than fiery liquor-based infusions. This is okay and even desirable. Just realize that you'll need to add more hot ingredients if you want an equal amount of heat. The process of cooking also can dial down heat levels. Once your syrup cools down a bit, taste it. If it's not spicy enough, cut a fresh, uncooked pepper and let it steep in the cooled syrup for 20 minutes or longer. You'll notice the heat levels perking right up!

A word of advice on simmering chile peppers: Some of the hotter varieties can exude a slight acridness into the air that can cause eye-watering, even coughing, for some people. Try to cook in a well-ventilated area.

SIMPLE SYRUP (BASIC)

Although you can buy premade simple syrup, a.k.a. *sirop de gomme*, it's much less expensive to make it yourself.

1 CUP WATER

1 CUP SUGAR

Combine the water and sugar in a small saucepan. Heat to a boil, continuously stirring until the sugar dissolves. Once the water starts to boil, lower the heat and allow to simmer, uncovered, for another 10 minutes. Remove from the heat and let cool to room temperature. Pour the syrup into a container and keep in the refrigerator.

HABANERO-INFUSED SIMPLE SYRUP

This versatile syrup is a standout in any cocktail. Try subbing serranos for habaneros, as used in the Aperol Spice.

1 CUP WATER

1 CUP SUGAR

2 HABANERO PEPPERS, CUT (OR MORE, IF DESIRED)

Combine the water, sugar, and habaneros in a small saucepan. Heat to a boil, continuously stirring until the sugar dissolves. Once the water starts to boil, lower the heat and allow to simmer, uncovered, for another 10 minutes. (The water may begin to take on a touch of color from the peppers.) Remove from the heat and let cool to room temperature. Strain with a fine-mesh sieve. Pour the syrup into a container and keep in the refrigerator.

CHIPOTLE-ORANGE SYRUP

Adapted from Janet Zimmerman, Atlanta. Chipotle pepper adds the smokiness of tequila; dried orange peel adds a flavor and aroma that mimics triple sec. Mix this simple syrup with lime juice and a splash of grapefruit juice in a salt-rimmed glass for the ultimate Virgin Margarita.

2 CUPS WATER

1 CHIPOTLE PEPPER

2 STRIPS DRIED ORANGE PEEL, OR FRESH PEEL, IF DRIED PEEL IS
    NOT AVAILABLE

¾ CUP SUGAR

Bring the water to a boil in a small saucepan. Reduce to a simmer and add the chipotle pepper and orange peel. Cover and let simmer for 15 to 20 minutes. Strain with a fine-mesh sieve and add the sugar. Return to a boil and stir until the sugar dissolves. Remove from the heat and let cool. Pour the syrup into a container and keep in the refrigerator.

SPICE SYRUP

Your kitchen will smell heavenly after brewing up this spiced, but not spicy, syrup. Try using it in the Spiced Tangerine Caipirinha for a tingly touch of spice and warm color. Omit the nutmeg, and this becomes Cinnamon-Clove Syrup, for the Aperol Spice.

1 CUP WATER

1 CUP SUGAR

1 TABLESPOON GROUND CINNAMON

1 TABLESPOON GROUND NUTMEG

1 TABLESPOON WHOLE CLOVES

continued

Combine the water, sugar, and spices in a small saucepan. Heat to a boil, continuously stirring until the sugar dissolves. Once the water starts to boil, lower the heat and allow to simmer, uncovered, for another 15 minutes. (The syrup will turn a cinnamon-brown color.) Remove from the heat and let cool to room temperature. Strain with a fine-mesh sieve. Pour the syrup into a container and keep in the refrigerator.

JALAPEÑO-MINT SYRUP

Combined with soda water and a squeeze of fresh lime, this simple syrup makes a great nonalcoholic mojito.

1 CUP SUGAR

1 CUP WATER

HANDFUL OF FRESH MINT (CRUSHED IN YOUR HANDS TO RELEASE ESSENTIAL OILS BEFORE ADDING IT TO THE POT)

1 JALAPEÑO PEPPER, SLICED

Combine the sugar, water, mint, and jalapeño in a small saucepan. Bring the mixture to a boil. Then lower the heat and allow it to simmer for 10 minutes. Remove from the heat and strain mixture. When cool, transfer to a tightly covered container.

Bitters

Many bitters have a tongue-tingling zing, but this tends to be muted when added to drinks, especially those with bold flavors. But they can really round out a drink and add a wonderful aromatic touch.

There aren't many spicy bitters on the market. One that isn't yet in wide release (but hopefully will be by the time this book comes out) is from a small company called Bittermans: spicy chocolate mole bitters. Also worth seeking out, more for spice than heat, is Fee Brothers Whiskey Barrel–Aged Bitters, which surrounds you with a wonderful cinnamon aroma when you dip your nose into your glass for a quaff.

SPICED ORANGE BITTERS

If you have some time on your hands, consider making your own orange bitters, dosed with a touch of anise and cardamom spice. The recipe below takes about a month from start to finish.

1 CUP GRAIN ALCOHOL

½ POUND DRIED ORANGE PEELS, FINELY CHOPPED

PINCH OF CORIANDER SEEDS

PINCH OF CARAWAY SEEDS

PINCH OF CARDAMOM SEEDS

4 TABLESPOONS NATURAL CARAMEL COLORING

Mix the alcohol, orange peels, coriander, caraway, and cardamom in a clear glass jar. Cover tightly and let stand for 20 days in a dark place. Shake the jar daily to agitate the contents.

Strain with a fine-mesh sieve into a clean bottle and close tightly. Put the strained seeds and orange peel into a saucepan and crush them with a wooden spoon. Just cover with boiling water and simmer for 5 minutes over low heat. Pour into a second jar. Cover and let stand for 2 days.

Strain this spice mixture and add the liquid to the first alcohol mixture. Add the caramel coloring. Stir. Strain again and let it rest until it settles perfectly clear.

GARNISHES AND OTHER HOT TOUCHES

Garnishes are like accessories for your drinks: small, decorative touches that enhance and amuse. Edible garnishes will add flavor, color, visual interest, and, perhaps, a touch of spice!

Classic Garnishes . . . With a Twist

Although there's nothing wrong with garnishing drinks with a wedge of lime or a curl of orange peel, some of the following ideas are perfect for adding flourish to spicy drinks:

Chile peppers. Fresh chile peppers always look great, whether dropped whole into a drink (which is best done with smaller pepper varieties) or sliced into rounds and perched on the side of the glass.

Get pickled. Marinated peppers such as Peppadew or pepperoncini also are wonderful additions, as are pickled okra, green beans, or carrot sticks.

Whole spices. Cinnamon sticks can be used as stirrers for coffee or other hot drinks; whole star anise looks lovely dropped into a champagne flute; orange slices studded with whole cloves can be floated on top of a party punch.

Olives. The martini's best friend is even punchier marinated in hot sauce or stuffed with piquant blue cheese. Try spearing olives and tiny red Thai peppers on a frilled toothpick; then balance the skewer across the top of a martini glass.

Fresh herbs. Sprigs of fresh basil, mint, or rosemary add an aromatic and attractive touch to juleps, mojitos, and more.

Meats. While unorthodox, small pieces of spicy pepperoni, mole salami, or other spiced meats can add a creative flourish to drinks. And they will help hungry drinkers muddle through until dinner, too!

Vegetable garnishes. A tall celery stalk, leaves intact, is the classic garnish for Bloody Mary–style drinks. But also consider cherry tomatoes or cucumbers—solo or with the edge moistened and rolled in hot pepper flakes for pizzazz and color contrast.

Spiced Glass Rims
Rimming glasses with salt, sugar, or spices provides an easy but impressive way to jazz up a fiery or classic cocktail with an extra-special, spicy touch.

Single ingredients for rimming glasses:
Salt, sugar (try colored or specialty sparkle sugars), finely crumbled gingersnap cookies (especially nice with sweet drinks; try using agave syrup or honey to adhere the cookies to the rim), Pop Rocks (really!), pulverized fireball candies, sour candy dust mix, or *li hing mui* powder. (Thank you to Martin Cate of Forbidden Island, Alameda, for recommending this finely powdered mix of dried plum and salt, which is popular in Hawaii for rimming margarita glasses.)

I don't recommend using cracked or crushed peppercorns alone to rim a drink glass, although I see it highlighted in recipes from time to time. You just get a disagreeable peppery mouthful. However, finely ground pepper mixed well with salt and other spices creates the right amount of piquancy.

To adhere salt, sugar, or spices to glasses, I prefer to use a splash of a liqueur used in the cocktail, so it doesn't interfere with the effect of the drink. But any liquid that moistens the rim will do. Some bartenders like to rub a wedge of lime or orange around the rim; others prefer to dip the edge in simple syrup, agave syrup, or even honey or grenadine. For an extra-spicy touch, muddle lime juice with a jalapeño slice and use the spiced juices to moisten the glass rim before inverting the glass in salt. Let your imagination be your guide!

Although you certainly can mix small batches for a single cocktail, mixing larger batches makes it easier to rim multiple glasses for large groups or parties.

CHIPOTLE SALT MIX

1 CUP KOSHER SALT

½ CUP CHIPOTLE CHILE POWDER

SMOKED SALT MIX

1 CUP SMOKED SALT

½ CUP KOSHER SALT

COCOA-CHIPOTLE MIX

1 CUP SWEETENED COCOA

½ CUP CHIPOTLE CHILI POWDER

TANDOORI SPICE MIX

This is used to rim the delightfully sweet-and-sour Tandoori Sunrise cocktail.

2 TEASPOONS SALT

2 TEASPOONS CAYENNE PEPPER

1 TEASPOON GROUND CUMIN

1 TEASPOON GROUND CORIANDER

1 TEASPOON PAPRIKA

1 TEASPOON GROUND TURMERIC

HAWAIIAN-SPICED BLACK SALT MIX

1 CUP BLACK HAWAIIAN SALT

⅓ CUP SUGAR

¼ CUP LEMONGRASS POWDER

⅛ CUP CAYENNE PEPPER

¼ CUP DRIED CILANTRO LEAVES

SUGAR AND SPICE MIX

1 CUP KOSHER SALT

½ CUP SUGAR

1 TABLESPOON GROUND CINNAMON

2 TABLESPOONS PAPRIKA

2 TABLESPOONS GROUND BLACK PEPPER

1 TABLESPOON CHIPOTLE POWDER

Other High-Impact Garnishes
ICE CUBES

Ice is a critical part of most cocktails. But we don't think often about ways to make ice more exciting. One option is to create decorative ice cubes by freezing a slice of fresh chile pepper, a lemon rind, or edible flower petals inside an ice cube. To make fancy ice cubes, freeze them in three stages:

1. Half-fill each compartment of an ice cube tray with water and allow the water to freeze.

2. Dip each decorative element (pepper round, etc.) into water and place one in each cube compartment. Return to freezer for a couple of hours.

3. Finish filling the trays with water and freeze until solid.

A second option is to add color and flavor to ice cubes by freezing simple syrup, fruit juice, or coffee or tea. (Don't bother trying to freeze liquor.) Here's a recipe for Spiced Ice Cubes that are used to add a bit of sizzle to an otherwise cool and classic gin and tonic.

TO MAKE ONE TRAY OF SPICED ICE:

1 HABANERO PEPPER, SLICED

3 CUPS WATER

3 CUPS SUGAR

8 SAFFRON THREADS, CRUMBLED

Combine all the ingredients in a small saucepan and bring to a boil. Stir until the sugar is dissolved, about 5 minutes. Allow to cool. Then remove the pepper and pour the liquid into an ice cube tray. Freeze until solid.

"GUNPOWDER" GARNISH

Add a dash of cayenne pepper on the top of a martini to create a "gunpowder" effect. Voilà! You now have a "gunpowder martini." You can try the same effect with a grate of fresh nutmeg, dark chocolate, or other flavors that complement the drink.

TECHNIQUES

The Rimming Technique

Set two plates or shallow glasses side by side. In the first plate, pour a tablespoon or two of liqueur. In the second plate, pour or mix up your spices/salt/sugar (a tablespoon or two will rim a couple of drinks). Invert the glass into the liqueur and just coat the glass rim. Lift the glass and set it down into the spice mix. (Alternatively, gently roll the outside edge of the glass in the spice mix.) Lift the glass out and set it right-side up to dry.

You can also do this ahead of time and carefully set glasses in the refrigerator or freezer to chill. This technique works best with cocktails that are made in a cocktail shaker; you can then strain them into your rimmed glass without disturbing your handiwork.

The Muddling Technique

"Muddling" is a bartending technique used to crush fruit, herb leaves, spices, chile peppers, and so on to release essential oils and juices. Often an abrasive, such as salt or sugar, is added to aid the muddling process. A mortar and pestle can be used for muddling. A sturdy glass or cocktail shaker also works and is the easiest way to muddle for a single drink. The other tool you'll need is a muddler, which looks a little like a small, blunt baseball bat with a bulbous end and is usually made out of wood or plastic. If you don't own a muddler, you can also use the back of a spoon to crush ingredients.

Crushed Ice Technique

It's traditional to use crushed ice in mint juleps to dilute the whiskey. If you don't have any on hand, wrap up a handful of ice cubes in a clean tea towel or in a plastic bag. (Be sure to squeeze out all the air or the bag will pop!) Grab a meat tenderizer and pulverize the cubes. Crushed ice melts quickly, so do this right before serving.

Making Layered Shots

It will take practice to get ingredients to layer properly. Start with the heaviest ingredients, and gently pour each successive layer over the back of a spoon to avoid disturbing the previous layer. But don't get too precious—even if you don't nail the layer effect, this shot still will taste the same!

Crushing Peppercorns

Get ready to take out all your aggressions. Pour a couple of tablespoons of whole peppercorns into a plastic bag. Squeeze all the air out of the bag, and seal tightly. With a meat mallet, small hammer, or the back of a spoon, pulverize the peppercorns. Pour out into a shallow bowl or plate for rimming glasses.

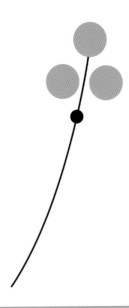

Drink Recipes by the Season

The drink recipes that follow are organized by season for easier reference and to highlight the use of fresh, seasonal ingredients.

Although it seems like virtually everything is available year-round, we all know that the cartoonish red strawberries that appear in grocery stores in January are faint shadows compared to the rich sun-warmed juiciness of berries sold at the local greenmarket in June. So just as we are relearning how to enjoy produce in season, bringing the same sensibility to drinks will only enhance the flavor and overall cocktail experience.

Hopefully, these recipes will encourage you to snip spring herbs from the window box and gather summertime melons, peaches, and blackberries to punch up your drinks. But each season—even when the last days of August fade into the cooler months and shorter days—brings its own spicy opportunities. Cool, crisp weather is perfect for smoky peppers and fall harvest fruits like apples and pears. And winter opens the door to a surplus of oranges, lemons, and other citrus fruits—as well as the excuse for richer, warming drinks spiked with ginger and clove to sip as the snowdrifts pile high outside.

spring

1

These are the drinks to turn to when nature finally comes out of hiding. Celebrate **springtime** with **fresh herbs** and **spices, bright flavors** and **fizzes**, and **light cordials** accented with **peppery flair.** Garnish the light flavors of **vodka, sake,** and **gin** with edible **flower buds** and sprigs of **fragrant herbs** from the window box.

WASABI-TINI

YIELD: 1 **DRINK** The cool green tint and pungent horse-radish zing make for a memorable cocktail, especially enjoyable alongside a platter of cucumber maki and other sushi rolls.

However, infuse with care. A cautionary tale told by one commercial distiller of wasabi vodka says it all: Since wasabi is a member of the mustard family, when combined with vodka (a volatile solvent), the end result is . . . mustard gas. The distillers had to wear gas masks while developing their wasabi-infused liquor.

1½ OUNCES WASABI-INFUSED SAKE OR VODKA (FACING PAGE)

½ OUNCE LIME JUICE

1 OUNCE GINGER ALE (OR MORE IF DESIRED)

1 SLICE CUCUMBER (SKIN ON), FOR GARNISH

1 MINT SPRIG, FOR GARNISH

Combine the sake and lime juice in an ice-filled shaker. Shake vigorously and strain into a chilled martini glass. Pour in the ginger ale to nearly fill the glass. Garnish with the cucumber slice and mint.

WASABI-INFUSED SAKE (OR VODKA)

1 TABLESPOON WASABI POWDER

8 OUNCES SAKE OR VODKA

Dissolve the wasabi powder in the liquor; shake well
before adding to the drink.

Want Extra Spice?

Moisten the edge of a cucumber slice and roll it in hot pepper
flakes. Use as a garnish on the edge of the glass.

PEPPERON-TINI

YIELD: 1 **DRINK** Where the standard "dirty martini" uses olive juice, this version gets extra heat and zing from pickled pepperoncini peppers.

3½ OUNCES CITRON VODKA

2 DASHES TABASCO GREEN-PEPPER SAUCE

½ OUNCE PEPPERONCINI JUICE

1 ROUND SPICY PEPPERONI, FOR GARNISH

1 WHOLE PEPPERONCINI, FOR GARNISH

Combine the vodka, Tabasco, and pepperoncini juice in an ice-filled shaker. Shake thoroughly and strain into a chilled, salt-rimmed glass. Garnish with a piece of pepperoni and pepperoncini speared on a toothpick.

GUNPOWDER GIMLET

YIELD: **1 DRINK**   Bang! This light and otherwise classic cocktail takes its name from a gunpowderlike dusting of cayenne pepper across the top of the drink, which can be omitted for drinking companions with tender taste buds. Props go to Presidio Social Club mixologist Tim Stookey of San Francisco.

2 OUNCES GIN

½ OUNCE ROSE'S LIME JUICE

PINCH OF CAYENNE PEPPER

1 LIME WHEEL (OPTIONAL), FOR GARNISH

Combine the gin and lime juice in an ice-filled shaker. Shake thoroughly and strain into a chilled glass. Gently dust the top of the drink with the cayenne pepper. Garnish with the lime wheel, if desired.

DIABLO

YIELD: 1 **DRINK** Diablo—Spanish for "Devil"—is a classic cocktail sassed up with fresh ginger and strong ginger beer. Crème de cassis, a black currant–flavored liqueur, imparts an appropriately deep, devilish hue.

1 ½ OUNCES SILVER TEQUILA

¾ OUNCE CRÈME DE CASSIS

½ OUNCE LIME JUICE

1 TABLESPOON PEELED, CRUSHED GINGER (OPTIONAL)

GINGER BEER

1 SLICE LIME, FOR GARNISH

1 SLICE GINGER, FOR GARNISH

Combine the tequila, crème de cassis, and lime juice in a cocktail shaker. Add the ginger, if desired, for a stronger flavor. Fill with ice and shake vigorously. Strain into a tall glass. Top off with ginger beer and garnish with a slice of lime and slice of ginger.

HOT SEERSUCKER FIZZ

YIELD: 1 DRINK This drink is adapted from Maria Polise at Sansom Street Oyster House in Philadelphia. It was a finalist in a cocktail competition sponsored by Clément Rhum, which I attended.

I watched curiously from the sidelines as the bartenders mixing up the drinks carefully removed the seeds from the jalapeño—and then equally carefully deposited a single seed at the bottom of a glass mixing cup—then proceeded to attack it viciously with a wooden muddler, mashing it into the bottom of the glass. The end result was a drink with moderate heat, tamed even more so by the addition of cream and egg white. Die-hard chile-heads may want to use a pepper ring with the seeds intact for extra sizzle.

1 JALAPEÑO PEPPER

2 OUNCES CLÉMENT PREMIÈRE CANNE

½ OUNCE CLÉMENT CREOLE SHRUBB

¾ OUNCE HEAVY CREAM

¼ OUNCE LIME JUICE

1 LARGE EGG WHITE

CLUB SODA

4 DASHES CINNAMON-HEAVY AROMATIC BITTERS (FEE BROTHERS
   WHISKEY BARREL–AGED BITTERS RECOMMENDED), FOR GARNISH

Cut a ¼-inch slice from the jalapeño. Deseed, reserving one seed. Crack the seed and jalapeño slice in a mixing glass with a muddler. Add the Clément Première Canne and Creole Shrubb. Add the cream and stir. Add the lime juice and egg white. Shake for 30 seconds. Add ice; shake for at least 1 minute. Strain into a large wine glass. Top with a splash of soda.

Garnish with the bitters.

NOTE Creole Shrubb is a delectable orange liqueur; Canne is white rum. Go for the real thing if you can find it, but now you know what to substitute if you can't.

SANGRIA SCORCHER

YIELD: 1 **DRINK** This sangria may look delicate, but don't be fooled by its appearance: It packs a good dose of heat. One of our drink testers referred to it as "a pink pit bull."

1 RED CHILE PEPPER, SLICED

2½ OUNCES WHITE WINE

1 OUNCE VODKA OR JALAPEÑO-INFUSED VODKA (PAGE 34)

1 OUNCE TRIPLE SEC

½ OUNCE LIME JUICE

⅓ OUNCE ELDERFLOWER CORDIAL

½ OUNCE CRANBERRY JUICE

1 TEASPOON DICED CUCUMBER

LEMON-LIME SODA

In a tall glass, muddle the chile pepper. Add a scoop of ice. Stir in the wine, vodka, triple sec, lime juice, elderflower cordial, cranberry juice, and cucumber. Top up the glass with lemon-lime soda.

SHIPWRECKED

YIELD: 1 DRINK An exciting variation on the traditional Dark 'n' Stormy was suggested by intrepid drink tester and cocktail enthusiast Diana Pittet. Gosling's is the traditional rum to use—Gosling's owns the trademark on the Dark 'n' Stormy name, meaning you can't use a different brand of rum and still call it by that name. But since this gingery zinger emphatically is *not* a Dark 'n' Stormy, feel free to use whatever brand of rum you like best.

3 COIN-SIZE PIECES PEELED FRESH GINGER

2 OUNCES DARK RUM

1 OUNCE DOMAINE DE CANTON GINGER LIQUEUR

4 OUNCES STRONG GINGER BEER

1 SLICE LIME, FOR GARNISH

In the bottom of a pint glass, use a muddler to crush the ginger and extract as much juice as possible. Add the rum and ginger liqueur and shake vigorously with ice. Strain into a tall glass half-filled with ice. Top the drink with the ginger beer and garnish with the lime slice.

THE HOT FLASH

YIELD: 1 **DRINK** A spicy, smoky margarita-style drink I concocted for the 2008 Tales of the Cocktail. It's made with reposado (moderately aged) tequila. Get it?

1 OUNCE GRAND MARNIER, PLUS 1 TABLESPOON FOR RIM

CHIPOTLE SALT MIX (PAGE 44) FOR RIM

3 OUNCES REPOSADO TEQUILA

1 OUNCE LIME JUICE

1 OUNCE POMEGRANATE JUICE

Moisten the rim of a glass with the 1 tablespoon of Grand Marnier. Roll the edge of the glass in the chipotle salt mix to coat. Allow to dry.

Combine the 1 ounce Grand Marnier, the tequila, lime juice, and pomegranate juice in a cocktail shaker with ice. Shake and strain into the rimmed glass.

NOTE This recipe is even better and hotter if the tequila is infused with fresh jalapeño peppers!

SPICED ICED TEA

YIELD: 1 **DRINK** A flash infusion of orange-spiked tea and hot peppers adds heat and bright flavor in a hurry.

1 TEA BAG (CONSTANT COMMENT OR OTHER ORANGE-FLAVORED BLACK TEA RECOMMENDED)

4 OUNCES VODKA

1 THAI CHILE OR SERRANO PEPPER, SLICED

2 OUNCES TRIPLE SEC

1 WHOLE PEPPER, FOR GARNISH

Immerse the tea bag in hot water for 10 seconds. Then remove it and immerse it in the vodka. Allow to steep for 5 minutes. During the last minute, add the sliced chile pepper. Remove the tea bag before proceeding.

In a shaker filled with ice, shake the infused vodka and the triple sec. Strain into a cocktail glass and garnish with the whole pepper.

RHUBARB COOLER

YIELD: 1 DRINK This libation combines the best of sweet, tangy-tart, and spicy-ginger flavors and is a luscious way to use in-season rhubarb. For more intensity, try muddling a few coins of fresh peeled ginger at the bottom of the cocktail shaker and then pour in the liquid ingredients.

1½ OUNCES GIN

1 OUNCE DOMAINE DE CANTON GINGER LIQUEUR

1 OUNCE RHUBARB PUREE (RECIPE FOLLOWS)

1 MINT SPRIG, FOR GARNISH

Vigorously shake together the gin, ginger liqueur, and rhubarb puree over ice, until frothy. Strain into a martini glass and garnish with the mint sprig.

RHUBARB PUREE

1½ CUPS 1-INCH PIECES RHUBARB

Puree the rhubarb in a blender and strain out the sediment through cheesecloth. (This can be done ahead of time. Just set aside the puree until you're ready to make the drink.)

MICHELADA

YIELD: 1 **DRINK** I was in Mexico City the first time I tried a Michelada, which is a beer-based cocktail. A colleague ordered a round for our group, and, at first, I declined: "I don't really drink beer." He pressed me to at least to try a sip. "Trust me," he said. "This is different." He was right. What was set in front of me was a light beer, tinged red with hot sauce and brightened with a margarita-style salt rim and the tang of fresh lime. My eyes must have betrayed my delight.

"*Delicioso, no?*" my friend prompted.

"*Muy delicioso—si!*"

1 WEDGE LIME, FOR RIM

COARSE SALT, FOR RIM

ONE 12-OUNCE CAN OR BOTTLE OF PILSNER-STYLE
    MEXICAN BEER, SUCH AS CORONA

1 LIME, JUICED

5 DASHES HOT SAUCE

5 DASHES WORCESTERSHIRE SAUCE

Moisten the rim of a tall beer glass with the lime wedge. Roll the edge of the glass in the salt to coat. Fill the glass with ice. Pour in the beer, lime juice, hot sauce, and Worcestershire sauce. Stir well.

PEPPADEW COCKTAIL

YIELD: 1 **DRINK**   If you've never had a peppadew, run out and buy some. These bright red South African peppers, usually sold hollowed-out and marinated, have an addictive sweet-and-spicy flavor that's perfect for a cocktail. That is, if you don't eat all of them straight out of the jar.

1 OUNCE PEPPADEW PUREE

2 OUNCES ABSOLUT CITRON VODKA

¼ OUNCE SIMPLE SYRUP (PAGE 38)

1 WEDGE LEMON (OPTIONAL)

1 WHOLE PEPPADEW, FOR GARNISH

Combine the peppadew puree, vodka, simple syrup, and ice in a cocktail shaker. Shake together and strain into a martini glass. If desired, squeeze fresh lemon over the top of the drink. Garnish with the whole peppadew.

NOTE: If you can't find peppadew puree, buy a 7-ounce jar of whole peppadew peppers, spoon out 3 or 4 peppers into a blender and puree.

THE FLAMETHROWER

YIELD: 1 DRINK The flame-bright vegetable mix makes about 2 to 3 glasses and can be served on its own in a pitcher for guests abstaining from alcohol. For an extra-special touch, ahead of time freeze a tray of ice cubes with red and green chile pepper rounds frozen inside (see page 46). Mix together regular and pepper cubes in each glass.

2 OUNCES TEQUILA

2 OUNCES VEGETABLE MIX (RECIPE FOLLOWS)

SQUEEZE OF LIME JUICE

1 WEDGE ORANGE

1 SLICE RED CHILE PEPPER

Mix together the tequila, vegetable mix, and lime juice in an Old-Fashioned glass filled with ice. Serve garnished with the orange wedge and chile pepper slice speared together on a toothpick.

VEGETABLE MIX

2 RED BELL PEPPERS, QUARTERED AND SEEDED

1 FRESH RED CHILE PEPPER, HALVED AND SEEDED

1 BUNCH RADISHES, CLEANED AND SLICED

¼ CUP ORANGE JUICE

Put all the ingredients in a food processor and puree.

JUMPIN' JULEP

YIELD: 1 **DRINK** Adapted from Danny Valdez, head
mixologist at Commander's Palace in New Orleans.
  Every year, on the first Saturday in May, the mint
julep is served at parties celebrating the Kentucky
Derby. This reinvention substitutes rye for the traditional bourbon. Says Valdez of the drink's superb
balance: "The jalapeño complemented the spice in
the rye; the sugar softened the spiciness; and the
fresh lemon brightened the drink."

7 MINT SPRIGS

1 SLIVER JALAPEÑO PEPPER

1 OUNCE SIMPLE SYRUP (PAGE 38)

1 WEDGE LEMON

2 OUNCES SAZERAC RYE WHISKEY

In a julep cup (or collins glass), muddle 6 mint sprigs
with the jalapeño. Add the simple syrup, squeeze in
the lemon wedge (and drop it into the cup), and add
the whiskey. Add a little crushed ice and stir. Add more
crushed ice to nearly fill the glass. Garnish with the
remaining mint sprig.

24-CARROT COCKTAIL

YIELD: 1 **DRINK** Created by Portland, Oregon–based consultant Ryan Magarian and served at Los Angeles restaurant Katsuya, this libation is made extra decadent with 24-karat gold flakes. But the fresh flavors and aromas of carrot, horseradish, and mint are gold medal–worthy, even unadorned.

6 MINT SPRIGS

1½ OUNCES HORSERADISH-INFUSED VODKA (FACING PAGE)

½ OUNCE LIME JUICE

2½ OUNCES CARROT JUICE

¼ OUNCE AGAVE SYRUP

Muddle the mint in a Boston shaker. Add the rest of the ingredients and ice. Shake vigorously and strain into a martini glass.

HORSERADISH-INFUSED VODKA

½ CUP CLEANED AND CHOPPED FRESH
   HORSERADISH ROOT

ONE 750 ML BOTTLE VODKA

Rinse the horseradish root thoroughly, place in an
infusion jar, and top with the vodka. Seal and let rest
for 24 hours. Strain with a fine-mesh sieve and bottle.

2 summer

In addition to the welcome seasonal surplus of **fruits** and **vegetables**, add a **hot pepper** plant or two to your garden. Look to **spiced punches** and **tropical libations** for the **Father's Day barbecue** and for the **Fourth of July blowout**, turbocharged **shooters**, or **cooling drinks** laced with the bright flavors of **ginger** and **mint**.

❋

SANGRITA

YIELD: 1 **PITCHER, OR ABOUT** 25 **TWO-OUNCE SERVINGS.** Adapted from Jacques Bezuidenhout, San Francisco. Prepare a pitcher ahead of time for your next summer party. Often confused with sangria, sangrita is a tomato-orange juice base with a swift mule-kick. While on its own, sangrita is nonalcoholic—and full of zesty flavors—it's traditionally accompanied by a shot of good tequila.

Some tough guys use sangrita as a toss 'em-back chaser for a tequila shooter; others recommend a daintier method of alternating sips—first the chilled sangrita, and then a mellow aged tequila.

½ CUP MEXICAN HOT SAUCE, SUCH AS CHOLULA

¼ CUP LIME JUICE

1¾ CUPS ORANGE JUICE

½ CUP GRAPEFRUIT JUICE

2 TEASPOONS SALT

1 TABLESPOON FRESHLY GROUND PEPPER

3¾ CUPS (30 OUNCES) TOMATO JUICE

1 JALAPEÑO PEPPER, STEMMED AND HALVED

ONE 750 ML BOTTLE AÑEJO TEQUILA

Combine all the ingredients except the tequila in a plastic or glass pitcher. Stir until the salt is dissolved. Allow the mixture to sit for 15 to 30 minutes and then taste for flavor. Add additional salt and pepper if desired. Remove and discard the jalapeño pieces when the desired level of heat is achieved. Chill the mixture until cold and then pour into 2 small tumblers. Serve each glass alongside a shot glass of añejo (aged) tequila.

HOT FUZZ

YIELD: 1 DRINK There's something about summertime that always makes me crave rum, and cooling daiquiris in particular. This peachy version, inspired by mixologist Adam Seger of Nacional 27 in Chicago, is a great way to use the surplus of super ripe peaches that arrive at greenmarkets and market stands in July and August, although frozen peach puree from the supermarket can be substituted in a pinch. (Seger's original recipe uses fresh mango as the star of the show.) Habanero-ginger syrup (one batch is enough for several cocktails) and fragrant spice powder further jazz up the drink.

1 TABLESPOON SUPER SEVEN-SPICE POWDER (FACING PAGE) FOR RIM

1 TABLESPOON SUPERFINE SUGAR FOR RIM

1 WEDGE LIME FOR RIM

JUICE OF 1 LIME

1 OUNCE RUM

1 OUNCE PEACH PUREE

¾ OUNCE HABANERO-GINGER SYRUP (FACING PAGE)

Chill a martini glass in the freezer ahead of making the drink. Mix together the seven-spice powder and sugar. Moisten the rim of the chilled glass with the lime wedge.

Roll the edge of the glass in the spice powder–sugar mixture to coat. Set aside.

Combine the lime juice, rum, peach puree, and habanero-ginger syrup in an ice-filled cocktail shaker. Shake vigorously and strain into the glass.

SUPER SEVEN-SPICE POWDER

2 TEASPOONS FRESHLY GROUND CINNAMON

2 TEASPOONS GROUND FENNEL

2 TEASPOONS DRIED GINGER

1 TEASPOON GROUND SZECHUAN PEPPERCORNS

1 TEASPOON GROUND CLOVES

1 TEASPOON GROUND STAR ANISE

1 TEASPOON GROUND CARDAMOM

Mix the ingredients together and keep in a tightly covered container.

HABANERO-GINGER SYRUP

1 CUP SUGAR

1 CUP WATER

1 HABANERO PEPPER, QUARTERED AND SEEDED

1 PIECE FRESH GINGER (ABOUT 3 INCHES LONG), PEELED AND SLICED THINLY

In a small saucepan, heat the sugar, water, habanero, and ginger to just below a boil. Remove from the heat and allow to steep for 5 minutes; remove the habanero pieces. Cool and strain, discarding the ginger. (The finished syrup keeps refrigerated for up to 3 weeks.)

LEMON-PEPPER MARTINI

YIELD: 1 **DRINK** Fresh homemade lemonade makes
a difference—but if you must cheat by using
commercially made lemonade (it's okay, we've all
done it!), grab a lemon wedge and squeeze it over
the top before serving for a fresh citrus aroma.
A raspberry or blueberry lemonade would add
beautiful color, too.

1 ½ OUNCES STOLI BLUEBERI VODKA
   (OR ANOTHER BERRY-INFUSED VODKA)

1 ½ OUNCES JALAPEÑO-INFUSED VODKA (PAGE 34)

2 ½ OUNCES LEMONADE

1 SLICE LEMON

FRESH BLUEBERRIES FOR GARNISH

Combine the vodkas and lemonade in an ice-filled
shaker. Strain into a chilled glass. Garnish with the
lemon on the side of the glass and drop a blueberry
or two into the center of the drink. Alternative garnish:
spear blueberries on a cocktail stirrer or toothpick and
balance on side of the glass. Float a lemon slice on top
of the drink.

CAJUN MARTINI

YIELD: 1 **DRINK** This simple and elegant drink was adapted from The Bombay Club, New Orleans. "This lives up to the martini name," one of our drink testers raved. "It's really cool and smooth, and the olives are a delicious treat." (We consumed a handful straight up—those olives are addictive!) Although The Bombay Club serves its signature hot martini with a mix of pepper and citrus vodkas, martini purists may prefer gin.

1 OUNCE JALAPENO-INFUSED VODKA (PAGE 34)

1 OUNCE CITRON VODKA

¼ OUNCE DRY VERMOUTH

2 TABASCO-SPICED OLIVES (RECIPE FOLLOWS)

Combine the vodkas and vermouth in a shaker with ice and shake vigorously. Strain into a chilled martini glass and garnish with the Tabasco-spiced olives speared on a decorative toothpick.

TABASCO-SPICED OLIVES

1 7-OUNCE JAR GREEN OLIVES WITH PIMENTOS (RESERVE A LITTLE OF THE OLIVE JUICE FROM THE JAR IF YOU LIKE YOUR MARTINIS HOT *AND* DIRTY!)

2 TABLESPOONS TABASCO SAUCE

Drain the brine from the jar of olives. Spoon the Tabasco sauce over the olives into the jar. Cover tightly and shake to coat the olives in the Tabasco. Allow to marinate in the refrigerator for at least 1 hour.

THE PRODUCE STAND

YIELD: 1 **DRINK** This savory, fresh, and colorful drink was inspired by Adam Seger of Nacional 27. It has its roots in the Bloody Mary but skips the vodka, subbing in *cachaça*, a distant cousin of rum. Raid the summer garden for cherry tomatoes and basil in season!

3 OR 4 CHERRY TOMATOES

2 WEDGES LIME

2 TO 4 FRESH BASIL LEAVES, PLUS MORE FOR GARNISH

2½ OUNCES TOMATO JUICE

2 OUNCES SAGATIBA PURA OR ANOTHER CACHAÇA

WORCESTERSHIRE SAUCE

HOT SAUCE

SALT

Muddle the cherry tomatoes and lime in a shaker. Add the basil, tomato juice, and *cachaça*. Then season to taste with Worchestershire sauce, hot sauce, and salt. Add ice. Shake well and serve in a tall glass garnished with basil or cherry tomatoes speared on toothpicks.

SPICY PISCO PUNCH

YIELD: ABOUT 12 SERVINGS Pisco punch is a San Francisco specialty dating back to the Gold Rush era of the late 1800s, so the golden hue of this punch is only fitting. Pisco is a brandy distilled from grapes, usually made in the wine-producing region of Pisco, Peru. Tim Stookey, a bar wizard with San Francisco's Presidio Social Club, jazzes up this version by infusing the Pisco with fiery Rocoto peppers, also native to Peru.

ONE 750 ML BOTTLE ROCOTO-INFUSED PISCO (FACING PAGE)

1 RECIPE PINEAPPLE SIMPLE SYRUP (FACING PAGE), PLUS
   RESERVED PINEAPPLE CHUNKS

1½ CUPS LEMON JUICE

1½ CUPS LIME JUICE

1 CUP PINEAPPLE JUICE

2½ TABLESPOONS PEYCHAUD'S BITTERS

Combine all the ingredients in a large punch bowl. Add a generous amount of ice to cool the punch and dilute the Pisco. (This is a very strong punch; dilution will be desirable.)

ROCOTO-INFUSED PISCO

½ ROCOTO PEPPER OR HABANERO PEPPER,
   CUT INTO SMALL PIECES

ONE 750 ML BOTTLE OF PISCO

Add the pepper pieces to the bottle of Pisco. Allow to sit overnight and strain.

PINEAPPLE SIMPLE SYRUP

3 CUPS CANE SUGAR

½ CUP WATER

½ PINEAPPLE, CUT INTO 1- TO 2-INCH CHUNKS (ABOUT 1 CUP)

In a small saucepan, bring the sugar and water to a boil, and simmer until the sugar is dissolved, about 3 minutes. Add the pineapple chunks and refrigerate overnight. The next day, strain and reserve the pineapple for the punch.

WATERMELON HOT

YIELD: 1 DRINK Much as melon-flavored liqueurs may try, there's nothing like the taste and aroma of fresh watermelon. Here it is accented with a bit of vanilla and chile pepper. In season, ripe watermelon is naturally sweet; if making this drink out of season, add an extra tablespoon of simple syrup to bring up the sweetness level.

3 CUPS FRESH WATERMELON CHUNKS, SEEDED

2 OUNCES SIMPLE SYRUP (PAGE 38)

½ TEASPOON FINELY CHOPPED FRESH GREEN THAI CHILE
   OR OTHER HOT CHILE

1½ OUNCES VANILLA VODKA

JUICE OF 1 LIME

SPRITE

Pulse the watermelon, simple syrup, and green Thai chile in a blender or food processor until combined. Set aside. (This will make several cocktails.)

Pour ⅓ cup of the melon-pepper puree, the vanilla vodka, and the lime juice into an ice-filled cocktail shaker. Shake and strain into a tall glass. Top up with Sprite. Serve with a straw (or two).

BLACKBERRY-POBLANO MARGARITA

YIELD: 1 **DRINK** The luscious purple color of this drink is a stunner! Taste a berry first to check for sweetness. If it's not supersweet, add a tablespoon of sugar when muddling the berries.

1 TABLESPOON FRESH BLACKBERRIES

1 TABLESPOON DICED POBLANO PEPPERS, OR 1 ½ TABLESPOONS, IF VERY MILD

1 OUNCE SILVER TEQUILA

¾ OUNCE COINTREAU

In a cocktail shaker, muddle the blackberries and poblano peppers. Shake with the tequila, Cointreau, and ice. Strain into a martini glass.

NOTE: If working with fresh blackberries, raspberries, or blueberries, to avoid pulp or seeds in your glass, strain before serving. Blackberries not in season? Use frozen berries.

SPICY CUCUMBER MARGARITA

YIELD: 1 **DRINK** This refreshing drink is tailor-made for sipping at a patio party on a hot afternoon because it's neither cloyingly sweet nor off-the-charts hot. However, go ahead and dial up the sweetness or heat levels if preferred.

½ CUCUMBER, PEELED AND CUBED

1 SLICE JALAPEÑO PEPPER, MINCED

1 OUNCE REPOSADO TEQUILA

½ OUNCE LIME JUICE

½ OUNCE TRIPLE SEC

1 SMALL PEPPER, FOR GARNISH

In a shaker, muddle the cucumber and jalapeño. Add the tequila, lime juice, triple sec, and ice. Shake and pour into a tall glass. Garnish with the small pepper.

Still Want More?

For added bite, mix chili powder with kosher salt. Rim the glass with the mixture before making the drink.

SUNBURNED BERRY

YIELD: 1 **DRINK** When summer raspberries are at their peak, grab an extra handful for this decadent drink with the bracing bite of chili powder mixed in. To take this to the "I dare you" level, rim the glass with a mixture of chili powder and sugar.

¼ CUP FRESH RASPBERRIES

½ TEASPOON CHILI POWDER

1 ½ OUNCES BOURBON

1 OUNCE SIMPLE SYRUP (PAGE 38)

1 OUNCE LIME JUICE

In the bottom of a cocktail shaker, muddle the berries and chili powder. Add the bourbon, simple syrup, and lime juice. Shake together with ice and strain into a martini glass.

KILLER KAMIKAZE

YIELD: 12 **DRINKS** Kamikaze shots take me back to college, when they were a staple at fraternity parties and the only alternative to skunky beer. Sure, you can be an adult and serve these shots on an elegant silver platter. But there's still only one socially acceptable way to down pepper-spiked shots: Toss back. Bellow loudly. Repeat.

2¼ CUPS PEPPER-INFUSED VODKA

2¼ CUPS TRIPLE SEC

½ CUP ROSE'S LIME JUICE

Shake the ingredients well with ice and strain the mixture into shot glasses.

ONE HOT PARTY SHOT

YIELD: APPROXIMATELY 15 **SHOTS** No longer just for rowdy college students, Jell-O shots have grown up, thanks in part to molecular gastronomy's influence on chefs and "bar chefs" to experiment with gelatinizing agents such as pectin and agar-agar. Our old friend Jell-O also gets the job done. Substitute half of the recommended water with a pepper-infused liquor, pour into small paper cups, and refrigerate until party time.

¾ CUP WATER

ONE 3-OUNCE PACKAGE LEMON JELL-O MIX,
    OR ANY FLAVOR YOU DESIRE

¾ CUP JALAPEÑO-INFUSED TEQUILA (PAGE 33)

3 JALAPEÑO PEPPERS, SLICED INTO ROUNDS

Bring the water to a boil. Pour the Jell-O mix into a bowl. Add the boiling water, stirring until the gelatin is dissolved, and then stir in the tequila. Refrigerate until cool but not set. Pour into shot glasses, molds, or small paper cups. Drop a round of jalapeño into each shot. Refrigerate until firm.

GIN AND TONIC WITH SPICED ICE

YIELD: 1 **DRINK** Infuse your gin. Sure. Infuse your tonic. Why not? But what about the ice? This cocktail is inspired by saffron-infused cubes served at New York's Pamplona restaurant, created by chef Alex Urena. But we've taken this to double-dare level by spiking the ice cubes with hot habaneros! For the gin, Old Raj is suggested; it's infused with saffron. Or substitute your favorite.

2 OUNCES GIN

4 OUNCES TONIC

4 SPICED ICE CUBES (RECIPE FOLLOWS)

Pour the gin and tonic over the spiced ice cubes in a tall glass. Stir and serve.

SPICED ICE CUBES

1 HABANERO PEPPER, SLICED

3 CUPS WATER

3 CUPS SUGAR

8 SAFFRON THREADS, CRUMBLED

Combine all the ingredients in a small saucepan and bring to a boil. Stir until the sugar is dissolved, about 5 minutes. Allow to cool, remove the pepper, and pour into an ice cube tray. Freeze until solid.

SPICY MINT MOJITO

YIELD: 1 **DRINK** Doesn't everyone love mojitos in the summertime? This one has a fabulous fresh-mint aroma, plus a refreshing jalapeño zing.

2 FRESH MINT SPRIGS

1 SLICE FRESH JALAPEÑO PEPPER

1½ TABLESPOONS TURBINADO SUGAR

1 LIME, HALVED

2 OUNCES LIGHT RUM

CLUB SODA

In a pint glass, muddle the mint (reserving one sprig for garnish), jalapeño slice, and sugar. Squeeze both lime halves into the glass, leaving one hull in the mixture. Add the rum, stir, and fill with ice. Top with the club soda, garnish with the reserved mint sprig, and serve.

COCO-GRENADE

YIELD: 1 DRINK A riff on the classic tiki drink, the sweet tropical flavors of crème de cacao, lime, and passion fruit are set against a bouncy backdrop of habanero.

1 OUNCE COCONUT MILK

¾ OUNCE LIGHT RUM

¾ OUNCE CRÈME DE CACAO

½ OUNCE MONIN PASSION FRUIT SYRUP

1 DASH ANGOSTURA BITTERS

½ OUNCE LIME JUICE

½ HABANERO PEPPER

If needed, liquefy the coconut milk by setting the can in 2 inches of hot water for about 10 minutes and then stir. Add all of the ingredients to a mixing glass, then fill with ice. Shake and strain into a hollow coconut. Serve with a straw; no garnish.

ALTERNATIVE SERVING SUGGESTION:
For a delicious frozen drink, blend the ingredients together with ice and then serve.

autumn

When the leaves begin to turn,
that's the perfect time to focus on the
smoky, earthy flavors of **chipotle,
ancho,** and **paprika** to highlight
harvest fruits like **apples** and **pears,
spiced pumpkin,** and **cranberries.**
Craft **spicy** signature drinks to
stir the **festivities** at Halloween,
Thanksgiving, and beyond.

THE ZAPPLE

YIELD: 1 DRINK Hot, sweet, sour, strong—this whiskey sour on steroids is a drink to warm the bones on a blustery late-autumn day.

1 OUNCE HABANERO-INFUSED APPLEJACK, CALVADOS,
 OR APPLE CIDER (RECIPE FOLLOWS)

1 OUNCE WHISKEY

½ OUNCE AMARETTO

¾ OUNCE LEMON JUICE

Combine the ingredients in a shaker with ice. Shake vigorously and strain into an ice-filled sour glass.

HABANERO-INFUSED APPLEJACK, CALVADOS, OR APPLE CIDER

1 HABANERO PEPPER, SLICED

1 CUP APPLEJACK, CALVADOS, OR APPLE CIDER

Steep the habanero in the liquor for about 2 hours and then remove the pepper.

HOT APPLE PIE SHOT

YIELD: 1 DRINK Hot Damn! Cinnamon Schnapps, an extra-kick-in-the-pants version of cinnamon schnapps made by De Kuyper, isn't always easy to find, but it's worth hunting down a bottle for spicy shots like this one. If you can't get a bottle, substitute Goldschlager or another brand of cinnamon schnapps—you'll still get a nice tingle after downing this pretty shot.

1 OUNCE GRENADINE

1 OUNCE APPLE LIQUEUR

½ OUNCE DE KUYPER HOT DAMN! CINNAMON SCHNAPPS
    OR REGULAR CINNAMON SCHNAPPS

½ OUNCE JALAPENO-INFUSED VODKA (PAGE 34)

Layer the ingredients in a shot glass, starting with the grenadine and ending with the vodka.

SMOKED APPLE

YIELD: 1 DRINK   One sip will make you forget those neon green appletinis seen on tired cocktail menus everywhere. Instead, this juicy drink plays up the smoky, earthy flavors of chipotle peppers and warm vanilla against a true apple background. (Add butterscotch to make a "caramel apple.") This is as good as autumn in a glass. If your pepper-infused liquor is especially potent, add a tablespoon of sugar or simple syrup to your cocktail to help mellow the rough edges.

1 OUNCE CHIPOTLE-INFUSED VODKA (RECIPE FOLLOWS)

1½ OUNCES VANILLA VODKA

2 OUNCES APPLE CIDER

½ OUNCE BUTTERSCOTCH SCHNAPPS (OPTIONAL)

1 THIN SLICE RED APPLE, FOR GARNISH

Combine the vodkas, apple cider, and schnapps (if using) in an Old-Fashioned glass over ice. Stir to combine. Garnish with the apple slice.

CHIPOTLE-INFUSED VODKA

2 OR 3 CHIPOTLE PEPPERS

ONE 750 ML BOTTLE PLAIN VODKA

Add the chipotles to the vodka. Allow it to infuse for at least a couple of hours and then remove the peppers.

PEPPERED POIRE

YIELD: 1 **DRINK** Poire William is a luscious, deeply aromatic pear liqueur. The problem with pear flavors is that they easily can become overpowering. But the zing of freshly cracked black pepper and the light fizz of sparkling wine help keep the pear flavors fresh and bright.

1 OUNCE GIN

½ OUNCE POIRE WILLIAM OR ANOTHER PEAR-FLAVORED LIQUEUR

¼ OUNCE PEAR PUREE OR SAME AMOUNT OF FINELY CHOPPED
   FRESH PEAR

½ OUNCE ELDERFLOWER SYRUP

2 BLACK PEPPERCORNS, CRACKED

SPARKLING WINE

FRESHLY GROUND PEPPER (OPTIONAL)

Combine the gin, pear liqueur, pear puree, elderflower syrup, and peppercorns in a cocktail shaker with ice. Shake well and strain into a champagne flute. Remove any bits of cracked peppercorn, if needed. Fill the remainder of the glass with sparkling wine. Finish with a good grind of black pepper if desired.

NOTE: Elderflower syrup is available in specialty stores.

APEROL SPICE

YIELD: 1 DRINK The rosy glow of bittersweet aperitif Aperol is warming enough on its own. But mixed with a duo of spiced syrups, this drink is a standout. If you prefer a spicier libation, double up on the serrano syrup and skip the milder cinnamon-clove sweetener. Angostura also has clove notes, so you'll still get the aromatic effect.

2 OUNCES APEROL

1 OUNCE GIN

½ OUNCE SERRANO CHILE SYRUP (RECIPE FOLLOWS)

½ OUNCE CINNAMON-CLOVE SYRUP (RECIPE FOLLOWS)

1 OUNCE LEMON JUICE

2 DASHES ANGOSTURA BITTERS

1 CINNAMON STICK, FOR GARNISH (OPTIONAL)

Combine the Aperol, gin, syrups, and lemon juice in a cocktail shaker with ice. Shake vigorously and strain into a cocktail glass. Add in the bitters and serve with a cinnamon stick, if desired.

continued

SERRANO CHILE SYRUP

1 CUP SUGAR

1 CUP WATER

2 SERRANO PEPPERS, SLICED

Combine all the ingredients in a small saucepan, uncovered. Bring to a boil, stirring to dissolve the sugar, then lower the heat and allow to simmer for 10 minutes. Cool and remove the peppers. Pour the syrup into a container with a secure cover.

CINNAMON-CLOVE SYRUP

1 CUP SUGAR

1 CUP WATER

1 CINNAMON STICK, BROKEN INTO PIECES

1 TABLESPOON GROUND OR WHOLE CLOVES

Combine all the ingredients in a small saucepan, uncovered. Bring to a boil, stirring to dissolve the sugar, then lower the heat and allow to simmer for 10 minutes. Cool and remove the cinnamon pieces and whole cloves. (Strain with a fine-mesh sieve if using ground cloves.) Pour the syrup into a container with a secure cover.

HERB BOUQUET

YIELD: 1 DRINK Celebrate the flavors of the fall harvest: cranberry, pear, almond, and rosemary. Consider serving this fragrant elixir to your Thanksgiving guests to sip while the turkey roasts.

2½ OUNCES ROSEMARY-INFUSED VODKA (RECIPE FOLLOWS)

½ OUNCE PEAR PUREE

½ OUNCE LEMON JUICE

¼ OUNCE ALMOND SYRUP

1 OUNCE CRANBERRY JUICE

1 ROSEMARY SPRIG, FOR GARNISH

Combine all the ingredients (except the rosemary sprig) in a cocktail shaker with ice. Shake well. Strain into an Old-Fashioned glass filled with ice. Garnish with the rosemary.

ROSEMARY-INFUSED VODKA

2 ROSEMARY SPRIGS

1 CUP VODKA

Roll the rosemary between your palms to release the fragrance and then add to the vodka. Cover and allow to steep for at least an hour.

THE BLOODY SCARY

YIELD: 1 PITCHER (10 DRINKS) Sure, you could garnish this Bloody Mary–style drink with traditional lemon wedges and celery sticks. But a gruesome fake eyeball or plastic spider will thrill Halloween partygoers as much as the sizzle of horseradish, hot sauce, peppers, and lemon!

ONE 46-OUNCE CAN TOMATO JUICE, WELL SHAKEN

¾ CUP LEMON JUICE

½ CUP WORCESTERSHIRE SAUCE

½ CUP BOTTLED WHITE HORSERADISH (NOT DRAINED)

¼ CUP HOT SAUCE

2 TEASPOONS CELERY SALT

1 TEASPOON RED PEPPER FLAKES

1½ TEASPOONS FRESHLY GROUND BLACK PEPPER

2 CUPS JALAPENO-INFUSED VODKA (PAGE 34)

10 PLASTIC SPIDERS OR 10 FAKE PLASTIC EYEBALLS, FOR GARNISH

Stir together all the ingredients, except the vodka and garnishes, in a large pitcher.

Fill ten 14-ounce glasses with ice and pour 3 tablespoons (1 jigger) of the vodka into each glass. Add the Bloody Mary mix and stir. Garnish and serve.

Rocking the Bloody Mary

Mary is one versatile gal. Created by bartender Pete Petiot while working at Harry's New York Bar in Paris, the Bloody Mary has evolved considerably since his original recipe (allegedly, simply mixed vodka, tomato juice, and ice). Consider varying any aspect of the traditional recipe to personalize your own Spicy Mary:

Juices: Tomato, Clamato, carrot, V8 . . .

Liquor: Vodka, gin, rum, *cachaça*, tequila, or whiskey

Liquid additions: Tabasco, A1 Sauce, prepared horseradish, pickle juice, barbecue sauce, balsamic vinegar, soy sauce, olive juice, lime/lemon juice, Angostura bitters, pepperoncini juice . . .

Creative seasonings: Cayenne pepper, fresh wasabi, ground cumin, hot or sweet paprika, red pepper flakes, onion powder, garlic salt, thyme, Chinese mustard, seasoned salt, chili powder, ground cardamom, Italian seasoning, ground ginger, Old Bay seasoning, basil leaves . . .

Seasoning mixes: Zing Zang, Arriba!, Demitri's, Forest Floor Foods, Original Juan, RedEye, your own special house mix!

Garnishes: Pepperoni, chorizo, spiced green beans, okra, stuffed olives, celery or carrot sticks, pickled vegetables, lemon wedges or peels, whole chile peppers, salted glass rim . . .

PUMPKIN PIE

YIELD: 1 DRINK On its own, this fall drink is mild, fragrant, and delicious. It's also a great blank slate—rim the glass with chipotle powder, and it becomes a spicy "Wow." Or finish the top with a froth of foamed milk and a chocolate syrup "spiderweb" for a sweet Halloween effect.

1 ½ OUNCES VANILLA VODKA, PLUS 1 TABLESPOON FOR RIM

1 TABLESPOON CHIPOTLE POWDER FOR RIM

2 ½ OUNCES MILK

1 OUNCE SPICED PUMPKIN PUREE

1 ½ OUNCES CRÈME DE CACAO

½ OUNCE ST. ELIZABETH ALLSPICE DRAM LIQUEUR

2 TABLESPOONS FROTHED MILK

1 TABLESPOON CHOCOLATE SYRUP

Moisten the rim of a glass with the 1 tablespoon of vodka. Roll the edge of the glass in the chipotle powder to coat. Allow to dry.

Combine the remaining 1½ ounces of vodka, the milk, pumpkin puree, and the liqueurs in a cocktail shaker with ice. Shake vigorously and strain into a martini glass.

Spread a thin layer of frothed milk on top of the drink. With chocolate syrup, dot the center of the drink. Draw a circle around the dot and a second, larger circle around the first circle. Use a toothpick or straw to draw the "web," starting from the center of the drink out to the edges.

SCOTCH BONNET

YIELD: 1 DRINK Take a sip, and then another. The flavor of this drink opens up beautifully. This masculine, almost smoky drink was created by Eben Klemm, the director of cocktail development for New York–based B. R. Guest Restaurants. Opt for a peaty Scotch for best effect.

2 OUNCES HABANERO-INFUSED SCOTCH (RECIPE FOLLOWS)

2 OUNCES PINEAPPLE JUICE

1 SPEAR PINEAPPLE, FOR GARNISH

1 HABANERO PEPPER, FOR GARNISH (OPTIONAL)

Stir together the habanero Scotch and pineapple juice in an Old-Fashioned glass. Add ice to fill the glass. Drop in the pineapple spear for garnish and serve.

HABANERO-INFUSED SCOTCH

1 HABANERO PEPPER, SLICED

1 CUP SCOTCH

Add the habanero to the Scotch. Allow to steep for at least 1 hour, then test for strength. When the desired heat is achieved, remove the pepper.

THE FIERY ALMOND

YIELD: 1 DRINK On a spicy scale of 1 to 10, the heat in this dessertlike drink rates a big fat zero . . . until you add the chipotle-cocoa rim. With this one easy but impressive touch, the spice level soars up to anywhere from a 7 to a sizzling 10! I recommend using a two-to-one cocoa powder to chipotle ratio, but use the chipotle solo if you dare.

¾ OUNCE AMARETTO, PLUS 1 TABLESPOON FOR RIM

1 TABLESPOON COCOA POWDER FOR RIM

½ TABLESPOON CHIPOTLE POWDER FOR RIM

½ OUNCE KAHLÚA

1 OUNCE LIGHT CREAM OR HALF-AND-HALF

Moisten the rim of a glass with the 1 tablespoon of amaretto. Combine the cocoa and chipotle powders. Roll the edge of the glass in the powder mix to coat. Allow to dry.

Shake together the remaining ¾ ounce amaretto and the Kahlúa over ice; strain into an Old-Fashioned glass half-filled with ice. Gently pour the cream over the back of a spoon to create a cream float on top without disturbing the rest of the drink.

ONE HOT MINUTE

YIELD: 1 DRINK Adapted from Jacques Bezuidenhout, San Francisco. This spicy tequila concoction took first place in a cocktail competition sponsored by the manufacturer of Tabasco hot sauce.

1 OUNCE CUCUMBER, PEELED AND PUREED

1 OUNCE UNFILTERED APPLE JUICE

1¾ OUNCES SILVER TEQUILA, SUCH AS PARTIDA SILVER

½ OUNCE LILLET BLANC

¼ OUNCE AGAVE NECTAR OR SIMPLE SYRUP (PAGE 38)

1 TEASPOON JALAPEÑO HOT SAUCE, SUCH AS TABASCO GREEN
JALAPEÑO PEPPER SAUCE

Combine all the ingredients in a cocktail shaker and fill with ice. Shake vigorously, strain into a highball glass, and serve.

CRAN-GINGER COBBLER

YIELD: 1 **DRINK** This fruity and fiery drink is inspired more by the bubbly fruit dessert than by the 1920s cocktail classic. You can omit the spiced rim and garnish with fresh cranberries floated on top of the drink.

2 OUNCES BRANDY PLUS 1 TABLESPOON FOR RIM

1 TABLESPOON BLACK HAWAIIAN SALT FOR RIM

½ TABLESPOON SUGAR FOR RIM

½ TEASPOON CAYENNE PEPPER FOR RIM

½ TEASPOON PAPRIKA FOR RIM

3 OUNCES GINGER ALE

1½ OUNCES CRANBERRY JUICE

1 OUNCE DOMAINE DE CANTON GINGER LIQUEUR

2 DASHES ANGOSTURA BITTERS

Moisten the rim of a glass with the 1 tablespoon brandy. Combine the salt, sugar, cayenne pepper, and paprika. Roll the edge of the glass in the salt mixture to coat. Allow to dry.

Combine the ginger ale, cranberry juice, the remaining 2 ounces of brandy, the ginger liqueur, and bitters in an Old-Fashioned glass. Add crushed ice until the glass is almost full. Stir well and serve.

THE CINDER

YIELD: 1 DRINK This drink was contributed by Phil Ward, mixologist extraordinaire at the New York speakeasy Death & Co. Combining equal parts salt, smoke, sweetness, and spice, this is a sophisticated, smooth drink for tequila lovers to savor.

1 OUNCE SIMPLE SYRUP (PAGE 38), PLUS 1 TABLESPOON FOR RIM

SMOKED SALT MIX (PAGE 44) FOR RIM

1 OUNCE JALAPEÑO-INFUSED HERRADURA SILVER TEQUILA (PAGE 33)

1 OUNCE HERRADURA REPOSADO TEQUILA

1¼ OUNCES LOS AMANTES JOVEN MEZCAL

1 OUNCE LIME JUICE

2 DASHES ANGOSTURA BITTERS

Moisten the rim of a glass with the 1 tablespoon of simple syrup. Roll the edge of the glass in the salt mix to coat. Allow to dry.

In a cocktail shaker, shake together the rest of the ingredients with ice, and strain into the rimmed glass.

FALL SPICE CORDIAL

YIELD: 1 DRINK Rich with the flavors of orange and vanilla and the caramelized goodness of bourbon, this drink falls more on the spiced than spicy side of the spectrum. This sweet cordial pairs well with autumn pies and other desserts or makes a great sipper to enjoy fireside.

1 OUNCE BOURBON

¾ OUNCE CHIPOTLE-ORANGE SYRUP (PAGE 39)

1 OUNCE VANILLA VODKA OR NAVAN VANILLA COGNAC

2 DASHES REGAN'S ORANGE BITTERS

ORANGE PEEL, FOR GARNISH

Mix together all the ingredients except for the orange peel. Shake together with ice and strain into a martini glass. Garnish with the orange peel.

MULE KICK

YIELD: 1 DRINK A variation on the classic Moscow Mule, this drink is powered by the heat of pepper-infused vodka. Choose a good commercial brand, or make your own.

2 OUNCES JALAPEÑO-INFUSED VODKA (PAGE 34)

2 OUNCES GINGER ALE

½ OUNCE ROSE'S SWEETENED LIME JUICE

1 SLICE JALAPEÑO PEPPER FOR GARNISH

Mix together the vodka, ginger ale, and lime juice in a glass. Add ice to fill the glass. Garnish with the jalapeño slice.

4 winter

Never mind the weather. Here comes an array of **sizzling cocktails** to keep you warm! Think of the delight of **spiced hot chocolate** and **eggnog** on overload; a **spiced sparkler** to ring in the **New Year**; and **fiery flavors** to **spice** up seasonal **citrus-driven** drinks.

MEXICAN HOT CHOCOLATE

YIELD: 1 **DRINK** Although it seems there are 101 ways to make Mexican hot chocolate, this is our favorite.

8 OUNCES MILK

1½ OUNCES BITTERSWEET CHOCOLATE, GRATED

½ TEASPOON MEXICAN SPICE MIX (RECIPE FOLLOWS), OR MORE IF DESIRED

1½ OUNCES KAHLÚA OR OTHER COFFEE-FLAVORED LIQUEUR

WHIPPED CREAM

1 DASH CHILI POWDER

Simmer the milk in a saucepan for about 1 minute, until heated through. Do not allow to boil. Whisk in the grated chocolate and spice mix, and continue to simmer until melted. Remove from the heat and stir in the Kahlúa. Pour into a mug or Irish coffee glass and garnish with a heaping spoonful of whipped cream. Dash a bit of chili powder on top.

MEXICAN SPICE MIX

1 TEASPOON CHILI OR CHIPOTLE POWDER

1 TEASPOON GROUND CINNAMON

½ TEASPOON GROUND CARDAMOM

½ TEASPOON GROUND GINGER

¼ TEASPOON GROUND CLOVES

¼ TEASPOON GROUND NUTMEG

Mix all the ingredients together ahead of time and cover tightly. Adjust the spices to your taste, such as more or less chili powder. This makes enough for 7 drinks.

DRAGONFIRE COCKTAIL

YIELD: 1 **DRINK** Don't let the sweet taste fool you—the heat in this drink packs a wallop! Although a few commercial hot pepper–infused vodkas are available on the market, it's very easy to mix up your own.

2 OUNCES JALAPEÑO-INFUSED VODKA (PAGE 34) OR TEQUILA (PAGE 33)

1 OUNCE TRIPLE SEC

1 OUNCE ORANGE JUICE

1 OUNCE LIME JUICE

1 LIME WEDGE, FOR GARNISH (OPTIONAL)

Mix together the vodka, triple sec, and orange and lime juices in a cocktail shaker filled with ice. Shake, strain into a tall glass, and garnish with the lime wedge.

NOTE To make a less-spicy variation on this drink, use unflavored tequila, and substitute 1 ounce habanero-infused simple syrup (page 38) in place of the triple sec.

SPICED TANGERINE CAIPIRINHA

YIELD: 1 **DRINK** Dosed with spiced simple syrup, this cocktail is aromatic, intensely colored, and full of bright citrus flavor. It's inspired by a drink that appeared on the menu at innovative restaurant Public, on New York's Lower East Side. If you can't find tangerines, try any type of orange. Tiny clementine segments work well.

3 SLICES TANGERINE

3 SLICES LIME

½ OUNCE SPICE SYRUP (PAGE 39)

2 OUNCES RUM

1 OUNCE GRAND MARNIER OR OTHER ORANGE-FLAVORED LIQUEUR

1 OUNCE LIME JUICE

Muddle 2 tangerine and 2 lime slices with the spice syrup. Add the rum, liqueur, and lime juice. Shake with ice and strain into a glass. Garnish with the remaining lime and tangerine slices.

THE PINK GRAPEFRUIT

YIELD: 1 **DRINK** Think pink—take advantage of the abundance of grapefruit available in wintertime! This drink is blushed with a hint of grenadine and fresh grapefruit. Omit the peppercorn rim if guests can't handle the heat; you'll still have a winning, refreshing drink.

1 OUNCE SIMPLE SYRUP (PAGE 38), PLUS 1 TABLESPOON FOR RIM

CRUSHED PINK PEPPERCORNS FOR RIM

½ LARGE GRAPEFRUIT, PEELED AND SEPARATED INTO SEGMENTS

2 OUNCES RUM

GRENADINE

Moisten the rim of a glass with the 1 tablespoon of simple syrup. Roll the edge of the glass in the peppercorns.

In a cocktail shaker, muddle the grapefruit segments and the remaining 1 ounce simple syrup. Shake with the rum and ice and strain into the rimmed glass. Add a splash of grenadine, just enough to give the drink a rosy pink tint.

GINGERED APPLE

YIELD: 1 **DRINK** I love spicy-sweet ginger in all its forms—fresh, pickled, sautéed, candied—and I love it just as much in a cocktail. This festive, gingery zinger is adapted from New York dessert impresario Pichet Ong and, like many great cocktails, is inspired by baking recipes. Think about how beautifully apples, vanilla, and ginger taste in pies and tarts. They combine just as beautifully in this drink. Pair with a slice of warm gingerbread or a plate of crackly gingersnap cookies.

1 TABLESPOON AGAVE SYRUP OR HONEY FOR RIM

2 GINGERSNAP COOKIES, FINELY CRUMBLED FOR RIM

2 OUNCES DOMAINE DE CANTON GINGER LIQUEUR

1 OUNCE VANILLA VODKA

2½ OUNCES APPLE CIDER

1 DASH LEMON JUICE

Moisten the rim of a glass with the agave syrup. Roll the edge of the glass in the crushed cookies to coat. Allow to dry.

Add the liquid ingredients to a cocktail shaker with ice and shake well. Strain into the prepared glass.

THE FIRESIDE

YIELD: 1 **DRINK** From Fahrenheit in Cleveland—on the luscious, gooey side, sweet and warm with cinnamon schnapps and chai spices. Pour this one into your favorite tea mug and savor on a winter evening!

1 TEA BAG SPICED VANILLA CHAI TEA

1 OUNCE GOLDSCHLAGER CINNAMON SCHNAPPS

1 OUNCE BAILEYS IRISH CREAM

1 TOASTED MARSHMALLOW, FOR GARNISH

Steep the chai tea in hot water and remove the tea bag. Stir together the chai, Goldschlager, and Baileys. Garnish with the marshmallow, and serve warm.

BANGKOK MARGARITA

YIELD: 1 **DRINK** Adapted from Pichet Ong's P*ONG restaurant in New York. Aleppo pepper is a Syrian red pepper with a bit of smokiness and just a faint touch of heat. Like its city namesake, the finished cocktail is sophisticated, exotic, and a little dangerous.

2 OUNCES REPOSADO TEQUILA

2 OUNCES PINEAPPLE JUICE

1 OUNCE DOMAINE DE CANTON GINGER LIQUEUR

PINCH OF MALDON SALT

PINCH OF ALEPPO PEPPER

1 LIME

Combine the tequila, pineapple juice, and ginger liqueur in a cocktail shaker filled with ice. Shake vigorously and strain into a martini glass. Sprinkle the salt and pepper on top. With a hand grater, grate lime zest over the top of the drink. Tap the grater lightly to release the zest and oil into the drink.

Aleppo pepper adds more savoriness than outright heat. For a spicier cocktail, substitute cayenne, ancho, or chipotle powder for Aleppo pepper.

BLOOD ORANGE–JALAPEÑO MARGARITA

YIELD: 1 **DRINK** This jalapeño-spiked margarita sizzles! Try this in winter, when blood oranges are in season, for a drink with a dramatic red hue. No blood oranges? No problem. Just substitute regular orange juice, plus a touch of pomegranate juice for color.

2 OUNCES JALAPEÑO-INFUSED TEQUILA (RECIPE FOLLOWS)

1½ OUNCES BLOOD ORANGE JUICE, OR 1¼ OUNCES ORANGE JUICE, PLUS ¼ OUNCE POMEGRANATE JUICE

½ OUNCE LIME JUICE

1½ OUNCES COINTREAU

In a shaker with ice, shake together all the ingredients and then strain into a margarita glass.

JALAPEÑO-INFUSED TEQUILA

1 JALAPEÑO PEPPER, SLICED

1 CUP SILVER TEQUILA

Add the jalapeño to the tequila. Cover and allow to steep for at least 2 hours. Taste to check the heat level; continue to steep for 1 more hour if a spicier tequila is desired.

AÑEJO MANHATTAN

YIELD: 1 **DRINK** Adapted from Ryan Magarian. The richness of aged tequila offsets the orange and vanilla flavors in the bitters and liqueur. Magarian garnishes this drink with a tequila-soaked dried cherry wrapped in spicy mole salami.

2 OUNCES AÑEJO TEQUILA, SUCH AS EL TESORO

½ OUNCE SWEET VERMOUTH

¼ OUNCE LICOR 43

1 DASH ANGOSTURA BITTERS

1 DASH REGAN'S ORANGE BITTERS

Combine all the ingredients in a pint glass. Fill the glass three-quarters full of ice. Stir swiftly for 30 seconds and strain into a cocktail glass.

RED DAWN

YIELD: 1 **DRINK** While this makes a fabulous brunch drink (hence the name), and it's less work than a traditional Bloody Mary, enjoy this harissa-spiked libation any time of day. Harissa is a Tunisian hot sauce or paste made with smoked chile peppers, garlic, olive oil, and spices like cumin or coriander. (Get harissa in a tube for longest shelf life.) Masochist alert: Double the amount of harissa if you dare!

2 OUNCES CITRON VODKA

4 OUNCES TOMATO JUICE

½ TEASPOON HARISSA

1 WEDGE LEMON, FOR GARNISH

Combine the vodka, tomato juice, and harissa in a glass filled with ice. Garnish with the lemon wedge.

"HOT LIPS" CHOCOTINI

YIELD: 1 **DRINK** Break this one out for Valentine's Day, or anytime you're looking to please your favorite chocolate-lover. Forget chocolate-covered cherries— for a fine finish, serve the drink with a chocolate-dipped red chile pepper on the side!

½ RED CHILE PEPPER, SLICED

¾ OUNCE JALAPEÑO-INFUSED VODKA (PAGE 34)

¾ OUNCE VANILLA-CITRUS LIQUEUR, SUCH AS NAVAN COGNAC OR TUACA

½ OUNCE KAHLÚA

FRESH CREAM

CHOCOLATE

In a cocktail shaker, muddle the sliced chile pepper. Add the vodka, liqueur, and Kahlúa. Shake with ice and strain into a pousse-café or martini glass. Gently pour cream over the back of a spoon to create a float on the top of the drink. Use a hand grater to add a generous amount of chocolate shavings on top of the drink.

HOT AND BOTHERED

YIELD: 1 **DRINK** According to Willy Shine, co-owner/ consultant of Contemporary Cocktails, this drink "will leave you hot and bothered." Do take care with flaming the grapefruit peel—although heating citrus oils imparts a wonderful fragrance and aroma, it's not an easy trick.

½ LEMON, QUARTERED

½ OUNCE GINGER HONEY

½ OUNCE CLÉMENT CREOLE SHRUBB

1 OUNCE PIMM'S

SPLASH OF GINGER BEER

1 GRAPEFRUIT PEEL

1 TEASPOON CAYENNE PEPPER

In a mixing glass, muddle the lemon, ginger honey, and Creole Shrubb. Add ice and the Pimm's and shake for 10 seconds. Strain into a chilled cocktail glass and charge with a bit of ginger beer.

Dredge the grapefruit peel in the cayenne pepper and flame over the cocktail.

TANDOORI SUNRISE

YIELD: 1 **DRINK** Tamarind is a sweet and sour fruit, here accented with an extra touch of Indian spice for the rim of the glass. Select brick-red Thai- or U.S.-produced tamarind pulp if you can find it—the darker color of Indian tamarind concentrate is less appealing in the drink.

½ OUNCE SIMPLE SYRUP (PAGE 38), PLUS 1 TABLESPOON FOR RIM.

1 TABLESPOON TANDOORI SPICE MIX (PAGE 45) FOR RIM

2 OUNCES SILVER OR BLANCO TEQUILA

1 OUNCE TAMARIND CONCENTRATE

½ OUNCE ORANGE JUICE

½ OUNCE DOMAINE DE CANTON GINGER LIQUEUR

Moisten the rim of a martini glass with the 1 tablespoon of simple syrup. Roll the edge of the glass in tandoori spice mix.

Combine the remaining ingredients in a shaker filled with ice. Shake vigorously and strain into the rimmed glass.

SPARKLING GINGER DAISY

YIELD: 1 **DRINK** A daisy is a classic juice-based cocktail sweetened with grenadine or a red liqueur, and often topped with sparkling wine. Here, the bright spice of ginger plays against a backdrop of bubbles for a festive holiday sparkler. And if you feel like gilding the lily, try one or both of the optional special touches below.

1 OUNCE PLYMOUTH GIN

1 OUNCE DOMAINE DE CANTON GINGER LIQUEUR

2 TABLESPOONS LEMON JUICE

1 TEASPOON GRENADINE

BRUT CHAMPAGNE

Combine the gin, ginger liqueur, lemon juice, and grenadine in an ice-filled mixing glass. Stir until well chilled, and strain into a champagne flute. Top with champagne.

OPTIONAL TOUCHES

- Rim the flute with sparkling sugar before pouring in the drink.
- Garnish with a cherry at the bottom of the flute.

"SUCKER PUNCH" EGGNOG

YIELD: 12 **SERVINGS** Although cocktails with egg whites are having a moment again, I prefer to use commercial eggnog as a shortcut for this holiday drink. Not only do I skip the risk of serving holiday guests a big cuppa salmonella, but if I'm going to fuss I'd rather spend my time tweaking the seasonings that make this nog a knockout.

1½ CUPS SPICED RUM, SUCH AS CAPTAIN MORGAN

7½ CUPS STORE-BOUGHT EGGNOG

FRESHLY GRATED NUTMEG

CHIPOTLE POWDER

12 CINNAMON STICKS

Combine the rum and eggnog in a decorative punch bowl, and whisk until frothy. Ladle each serving into punch cups or teacups, and garnish with a dash of nutmeg, a pinch of chipotle powder, and a whole cinnamon stick to stir.

resources

In addition to well-stocked specialty and ethnic grocery stores, the following sources can help you find a wealth of spicy supplies for cocktail and other recipes.

Bendistillery—For Mazama-Infused Pepper Vodka and other small-batch spirits.

www.bendistillery.com or 541-318-0200

Chile Pepper magazine—A fun and fiery read. Treat yourself to a subscription.

www.chilepepper.com or 866-378-2951

Cross Country Nurseries—A huge selection of chile and sweet pepper plants.

www.chileplants.com

FireGirl.com—For hot sauces and fun descriptions. Their tagline says it all: "Hike naked; splash through puddles; put hot sauce on all your food."

www.firegirl.com

HotSauce.com—For Frostbite and other hot sauces; super-fast delivery.

www.hotsauce.com or 877-WWW-SAUCE

Kalustyan's—For spices, hot sauces, and pickled peppers from around the world, and a wide selection of cocktail bitters.

www.kalustyans.com or 800-352-3451

Modern Spirits—For celery peppercorn, candied ginger, and other specialty vodkas.

www.modernspiritsvodka.com or 626-771-9469

Rancho Gordo—For fresh chile peppers in season and dried chiles year-round.

www.ranchogordo.com or 707-259-1935

index

Index

Liquid Measurements

Bar spoon =	½ ounce
1 teaspoon =	⅙ ounce
1 tablespoon =	½ ounce
2 tablespoons (pony) =	1 ounce
3 tablespoons (jigger) =	1½ ounces
¼ cup =	2 ounces
⅓ cup =	3 ounces
½ cup =	4 ounces
⅔ cup =	5 ounces
¾ cup =	6 ounces
1 cup =	8 ounces
1 pint =	16 ounces
1 quart =	32 ounces
750 ml bottle =	25.4 ounces
1 liter bottle =	33.8 ounces
1 medium lemon =	3 tablespoons juice
1 medium lime =	2 tablespoons juice
1 medum orange =	⅓ cup juice